CELG

# BONO

Center Point
Large Print

Also by Helen Brown and available from Center Point Large Print:

*Cats & Daughters*

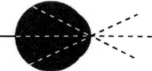

**This Large Print Book carries the Seal of Approval of N.A.V.H.**

# BONO

## THE AMAZING STORY OF
## A RESCUE CAT
## WHO INSPIRED A COMMUNITY

# HELEN BROWN

CENTER POINT LARGE PRINT
THORNDIKE, MAINE

This Center Point Large Print edition
is published in the year 2018 by arrangement with
Kensington Publishing Corp.

Copyright © 2018 by Helen Brown.

The text of this Large Print edition is unabridged.
In other aspects, this book may vary
from the original edition.
Printed in the United States of America
on permanent paper.
Set in 16-point Times New Roman type.

ISBN: 978-1-68324-844-6

Library of Congress Cataloging-in-Publication Data

Names: Brown, Helen, 1954- author.
Title: Bono : the amazing story of a rescue cat who inspired
    a community / Helen Brown.
Description: Center Point large print edition. | Thorndike, Maine :
    Center Point Large Print, [2018]
Identifiers: LCCN 2018015878 | ISBN 9781683248446
    (hardcover : alk. paper)
Subjects: LCSH: Brown, Helen, 1954- | Cat owners—United States—
    Biography. | Foster care of animals. | Large type books.
Classification: LCC SF442.82.B76 A3 2018 | DDC 636.80092/9—dc23
LC record available at https://lccn.loc.gov/2018015878

For Philip and my sister, Mary Dryden

*Do not be afraid to love me.*
*If I break your heart, it will open again.*
*And you will be more alive.*

# CONTENTS

# BONO

## Chapter One

# PLAID PAJAMAS

*A cat must embrace every
one of her nine lives.*

There's no law against flannelette pajamas as far as I know. This particular pair was dark green plaid, however, and identical to the ones Dad wore through his later years.

Not only that, they were out of season. We were sweltering through a particularly hot summer. Winter weight nightwear was the last thing he needed.

"What do you think?" Philip said, swaggering into the bedroom with the nonchalance of a seasoned fashion model.

I adjusted my head on the pillow so I could finish the crossword without the assistance of a neck brace.

How could I tell my beloved husband that, without realizing it, he was mutating into my father?

It didn't take Sherlock Holmes to work out what had happened. Philip had been wandering through a department store during one of his lunch breaks when some shop assistant sniffed him out as easy prey.

Blonde, 25, and with teeth that would have bankrupted her parents, she'd have beckoned him over to stroke the fabric. Helpless as a terrier in front of a plate of fillet steak, he would have trotted through the underwear displays to her counter. She would have beamed up at him and stroked last winter's flannelette with her manicured talons. He would have been mesmerized as she pointed out the white piping edging on the collar and flattered him into believing it was retro. Honestly, straight men should be banned from shopping alone.

My husband of twenty-two years is an exceptionally kind and tactful man. He has never once grumbled about the oversized T-shirts I wear to bed (100 percent cotton, the only type that breathes properly) or the accompanying beige granny pants (giant knickers finishing at the waistline are the world's best kept secret).

A sensible woman would have rolled onto her side and completed the crossword ("10 Down: Cooking fat (4)"). But common sense has never been my forte. I had to open my mouth and say the new pajamas weren't very exciting. In no way was I making fun of him. I was just talking the way people do once we've nudged past 50. The instant the words rolled off my tongue I regretted them. He had every right to retaliate with observations about the extra twenty pounds I'd piled on while writing the last book, or point out that my idea of clothes storage is to toss them on the floor.

But he just smiled in that understated way that

has always intrigued me. "Be careful what you wish for," he said, lifting his side of the quilt and climbing in beside me. "Excitement has a price."

The words hit me with the force of a cast iron wok landing on my head. Grateful as I was for our marriage, the wonders of modern medicine, our grown-up kids, and two beautiful granddaughters, in recent months I'd fallen into a confusing state of restlessness. Our life together had begun to feel a little, well, ho-hum. Excitement may come at a price, but I was almost ready to pay it.

My life hadn't always seemed so dull. Nothing could surpass the ecstasy of gazing into the faces of my four children for the first time. On countless occasions, a burst of bliss had popped out unexpectedly from the dampness of a kitten's nose, or the cool caress of grass under my feet. But the life I'd once led as a journalist, rubbing shoulders with the likes of Mick Jagger and Paul McCartney, seemed a million moons ago. In those days, I could pick up a phone to hear some PR person begging me to do a one-on-one interview with Pavarotti or to take a trip to Alaska or Tahiti for the price of a few lines of travel writing.

These days, I was resorting to frankly desperate measures for a bit of excitement, and it wasn't working—for me or anyone else. The purple streak I'd persuaded the world's longest suffering stylist, Brendan, to apply to my fringe had been a disaster. Though Philip and the family were too tactful to say anything, I was starting to realize the new red fishnet stockings were a joke. Every day was a duller replica of the last. On my morning walk to the shopping center, a once opalescent sky bore down like a steely battle helmet. The magpies that used to land at my feet had, with the careless freedom only birds can muster, fluttered off to some other neighborhood. Even the birds were bored with me.

A visit to the doctor was an option, but I knew she'd reach for her prescription pad and tell me to exercise more. I had no intention of joining the army of medicated women with their fake smiles and dilated pupils concealing their shattered emotional states.

If I'd been in a novel, I might have taken off to France to embark on an affair with a lavender farmer. But even if I could do that to Philip, what self-respecting lavender farmer would have me? He'd laugh at my schoolgirl French and hate me for scattering croissant crumbs over his bespoke stone floor.

Instead, to liven things up on one slow Sunday afternoon, I smashed a serving bowl. I've never been a plate thrower. It landed with a satisfying wham at the same time I realized I'd actually quite liked that bowl. It was white porcelain, German, with delicate wavy edges, probably irreplaceable. My old self would have chosen to break something cheap and dispensable, like one of Jonah's feeding dishes. But that nice woman, who would have been too dignified and aware of others' feelings to throw anything heavier than a sock, had vanished. In her place had appeared a madwoman.

The only thing more shocking than the sound of china exploding on floor tiles was Philip's face. His skin went pale. His lips formed a circle. In the hollow silence, I was certain he would grab his car keys and walk out the door. He had every right to. I almost wished he would—I was tired of worrying about him leaving me for being too old, too fat, too me-ish anyway.

Gazing down at the shards of broken porcelain, I waited. Seconds later, I watched shamefaced as he reached for the dustpan and scraped the wreckage off the floor.

Our marriage was by no means on the rocks. If anything, our connection had deepened following a recent brush with breast cancer. During those months after the surgery, we'd clung to each other like a pair of shipwrecked sailors. Once things had settled down, however, and we adjusted to the idea I wasn't about to snuff it, we morphed into well-meaning neutrality. Like conjoined sleepwalkers, we drifted through routines of coffee drinking and sitting in front of the fire with matching iPads. There was Jonah, too, of course. Our deranged, medicated Siamese expected me to devote every waking moment to him.

My prognosis was good. But while I'd been relieved of the burden of arranging my own funeral in a hurry, part of me was missing the intensity of teetering on the edge.

If experience had taught me anything it was to be wary of irrational impulses. Decades earlier, a similar concoction of hormonal overdrive had catapulted me into teenage marriage and motherhood at the age of 19. Still, after my speed date with death, I couldn't help feeling that however much sand was left in the hourglass, I wanted to spend it living as if I was dying. I wanted to seize life with all its dangerous beauty and vitality.

Philip removed his glasses and put them on top of the pile of books on his bedside table. He leaned over, planted a kiss on my nose, and snuggled under the sheets. We always went to bed at 9:30 on Sundays because of the Big Week Ahead. He would be up at dawn pummeling away on his exercise bike before jumping into the shower. After he had shaved and climbed into his suit, he would bring me a mug of tea with toast and raspberry jam. Life together was cozy, but numbingly predictable.

My pen hovered over "7 Across: Boredom" (five letters beginning with *E*). Distant thrumming from down the hallway interrupted my concentration. The drumroll of paws pummeling floorboards was accompanied by a series of urgent and increasingly loud yowls.

"Here we go," Philip muttered from under the covers.

Clutching the crossword book, I tensed my buttocks and prepared for the assault. Seconds later, a wild-eyed Siamese burst through the bedroom door, sailed through the air, and landed with a thud between my legs.

My husband took a dim view of Jonah's fixation with my thighs. Whenever I tried to explain my nether regions have a well-upholstered squishiness that's irresistible to a comfort-loving feline, he seemed unconvinced. I didn't go out of my way to reassure him. Not when he and Jonah were the only two males on Earth who expressed any interest in my anatomy.

Damp and triumphant from battling imaginary dragons in his outdoor catio, Jonah emitted a victorious meow. He turned around three times, burrowed between my legs, and kneaded the quilt cover. Once he was confident I was satisfactorily pinned to the bed, the cat draped his ridiculously long tail over the mound of my knees. I lowered my hand and massaged his velvety nose with my forefinger. Purring like a tractor, he flossed his teeth on the other available fingertips.

Jonah flashed me a sapphire blink from behind his dark chocolate mask. He clucked appreciatively, and yawned. I lay still and waited for him to doze off. When the purring faded to a gentle rattle, I figured it was safe to reclaim my hand. I tried to inch it away, but a proprietorial paw stretched across my wrist. Jonah unsheathed his claws and squeezed my skin without *quite* puncturing it—his way of reminding me my status was several notches below his. Still, there's nothing more flattering than a cat including you in his life, even if he regards you as little more than a mobile cushion.

With Philip on one side and Jonah wedged between my legs, I felt like the filling in an alpha male croissant. Much as I loved Jonah, he was the most demanding cat in the world. A Velcro cat, he clung to my lap, my arms, my neck, and never let me out of his sight. He bellowed like a moose when things weren't going his way, which seemed to be most of the time these days.

Once they'd settled in and were drifting into their parallel dream worlds, I started to retrieve my hand inch by inch. With Jonah anchoring me to the mattress, I reached for the bedside light. My body emitted an involuntary groan, part of a symphony of noises it was making by itself these days.

Staring into the darkness, I wondered what was going on inside my husband's head. He seemed to have transitioned from the high passion of our early years to midlife contentment with hardly a glitch. Either that or he was an actor of Oscar-winning potential.

I supposed it was inevitable that French kisses should morph into Sunday night pecks. Love has many layers. Sex can be transporting and addictive, but to lust after the same person over and over again is asking a lot of the imagination.

Movies make a big deal of the first kiss and rapturous nights in bed together, followed (ninety minutes later) by the frantic dash to the airport when he thinks she's leaving him. Hollywood seems to have little interest in portraying the everyday and astonishing achievement of sustaining love through all the reincarnations two people go through in a lifetime together.

His breathing was becoming deep and regular.

"What do you want?" I asked.

"Whaaa?!" he said, tugging the sheet over his shoulder, and encasing himself like a caterpillar. "A good night's sleep wouldn't go amiss."

"No, I mean it," I said, tapping his shoulder. "If you had just a few years left, how would you choose to spend them? Is there something you've always dreamed of, a place you've wanted to go?"

The room fell silent. He'd either fallen asleep, or was thinking.

"Antarctica," he said after a long pause.

He knew my theory on Antarctica. Some places on Earth are so sacred people should leave them alone. Besides which, I can't stand the cold.

"And . . . ?"

"A shack by the sea, and maybe a little boat to knock about in."

He'd always talked about having a beach house, but I could think of nothing worse. Being in charge of two kitchen sinks, having double the number of beds to make and a house full of sand sounded like slavery. As for boats, I hadn't earned the title of Vomit Queen for nothing.

Jonah stirred and made licking sounds. A ball of panic settled in the back of my throat. It wasn't so much that my life was nearly over, but that I might have chosen the *wrong* life. There was every chance this restlessness was nothing to do with second adolescence but a sign I was wasting my days cooking dinners and sifting through the litter box of an imperious cat. Maybe my soul—if I had one—was telling me I didn't belong in a ramshackle house on a dead-end street in inner Melbourne, and that my *real* home was somewhere altogether more glamorous?

At first, the voice in my ear sounded like tinnitus, but the message grew loud and clear:

*Time's running out. Grab all the excitement you can.*

I sank into a whirlwind of turbulent dreams. Since I'd opened up to the idea of excitement, it seemed to be rushing in with cyclonic force. Though I'd never experienced a super storm, I'd seen how the one called Sandy had engulfed Manhattan a few months earlier. Watching the televised images of waves swallowing up the city moved me deeply. At the time, I had no idea that hurricane's force was far from spent. It would soon be driving another form of tumult into my life. I needn't have worried about lack of adventure. In an animal shelter across the world, a bundle of excitement was sitting inside a cage, licking its fluffy black paws . . . and calling across space and time to me.

## Chapter Two

# HEAVEN OR HELLHOLE

*A feline is seldom what she seems.*

The following morning, I woke with a plan so perfectly formed it practically qualified as a vision. If it were true that I'd ended up in the wrong life in the wrong city, I'd change it, at least for a little while. And where better to move to than New York?

After all, New York and I had unfinished business. Though I'd never lived among the city's skyscraper canyons, I'd spent a tantalizing time there a few years earlier celebrating the launch of my first book, *Cleo*. The parties were every bit as glittering as I'd dreamed, the people warm and fascinating.

No one had been more surprised than me when *Cleo* bounced onto the *New York Times* bestseller list. For one thing, the book was about a cat and how she'd helped our family heal after my nine-year-old son Sam was run over and killed in 1983.

While Cleo the cat seemed to be an angel from another world through the darkest days of my grief, when I sent her story to literary agents and publishers most had run for the hills. Eventually it was picked up and before long it had been translated into countless languages.

Just when I was thinking it was time to sign

up for gardening classes, I was spinning around the world in a whirl of happy disbelief—magical parties in Frankfurt and Vienna, where writers are revered as artists. In Warsaw, Poland, I found people love to read so much they fill a soccer stadium for their book fair. A tour of the tsunami region of Japan affected me profoundly. It was an honor beyond words when people who had lost so much wanted to share their grief with me.

At an elegant lunch on a whirlwind trip to New York, I steadied a glass of chardonnay and hoped my antipodean earthiness and oversized feet weren't too laughable.

Across the table, a woman beamed worldly warmth from under a froth of blond hair. The bright scarf around her neck was pinned together with a vivid enamel brooch the shape of a cat. Feline fanatic to the core, she confessed to keeping three cats in her two bedroomed apartment. When she smiled, the restaurant took on a peachy hue. Her name was Michaela Hamilton, executive editor at Kensington Publishing, and *Cleo*'s US editor.

Now, with a new book soon to be released in the United States, I had a watertight excuse to return to New York. Except this time, I'd stay longer, immerse myself in the city, and put my dreary suburban life on hold. If I met enough fabulous people, some of their glamour might rub off on me. I'd drink champagne with the literati and (if my knee held out) dance down Fifth Avenue at dawn. They might even like me enough to ask me to stay on indefinitely. Only a fool would say no to that. All I had to do was contact Michaela and introduce my other half to the brilliance of the idea.

Philip's side of the bed was empty. I knew the rule. I was supposed to stay put until he brought in the tea and toast. Our sleepy cat protested as I rolled him off my body and leapt out of bed into my dressing gown. Jonah yowled and tried to cut me off so he could wrangle me back to bed for his regular cuddle. I sidestepped the flicking tail and dashed into my study.

According to my calculations, it would be late afternoon in New York.

I was in luck. Michaela was still at her desk.

Her enthusiasm bubbled back across cyberspace. If I visited in a couple of months' time, toward the end of March, to coincide with the release of *Cats & Daughters*, we could have fun together and maybe sell a few books. She agreed that instead of staying in a hotel I should rent an apartment. That way it would be easier to extend my stay and discuss new projects with her.

I pictured myself trotting across Times Square to her office building every morning to discuss my outline for the next *Game of Thrones* before heading around the corner to binge on a Broadway matinee. As dusk settled over the Empire State Building I'd make a cameo appearance on *The Daily Show*, before heading across town for cocktails with Stephen Colbert. It was like offering an ice addict her own meth lab.

After Michaela and I signed off, I floated into the kitchen, where Philip was applying broad strokes of jam to a slab of toast.

"What's up?" he asked.

I wasn't sure how to share the news. Jonah snaked around my ankles and wailed like Plácido Domingo.

"Has he had his pill?" I asked. Without his daily antipsychotic medication, our cat screams nonstop, shreds the house to pieces, and (if all else fails) goes on a spraying jag.

Philip is the resident expert at pill dispensing. Jonah lies like a baby in his arms while he drops the capsule deftly in the back of the feline's throat. Whenever Philip's away and I'm forced to man the pill, the patient wriggles, spits the thing out, and snubs me for hours.

"I gave it to him just now," he said. "Aren't you cold?"

"No, I'm quite hot, actually. Well, I used to be. I was thinking . . ."

"Why don't you go back to bed? I'll bring this in to you."

"I'm thinking . . . I've got to go to New York."

The words came out with the elegance of a cat coughing up a hair ball.

"What for?"

"They want me there to promote the new book," I said.

My husband took a yellow dishcloth from the bench top and wiped the red tear dribbling down the side of the jam jar.

"The ants are back," he said after a long silence.

I was so over the ants. They swarmed Jonah's food bowls every night. He's terrified of ants, which is undignified for a cat who relished the idea of taking on a rat, or even a small dog. We'd tried every type of trap and poison, but our ants just ignored them and went on with their plans to take over the world.

Drowning ants was my job. I went to the laundry, where the food bowls had transformed overnight into hillocks of writhing life. I filled the yellow bucket from the cold tap and plunged the bowls into the water. Somber with guilt, I watched their bodies form dark swirls as they spiraled down the drain.

"So how long do you want to be away for?" Philip called out.

I returned to the kitchen, where he presented me with a plate of toast.

"I'm not sure," I said, sinking my teeth into the crust.

Philip said nothing.

"Why don't you come along?" I asked. "You could take a year off."

I knew what the answer would be. He could hardly expect the firm to keep his job open while he gallivanted around the world with me for twelve months. Aside from the fact he was too young to retire, our nest egg was barely fertilized.

I waited for him to negotiate my absence down to two weeks, or maybe three. Instead, he put the jam jar in the fridge where the ants couldn't get it and padded upstairs toward his study.

"Where are you going?" I asked, feeling a stab of alarm.

"To see what flights I can get you on," he called over his shoulder. "How long do you want to be away for, did you say?"

How much time would it take to stop feeling this empty and confused? A month, a year . . . forever?

"Depends how much stuff they need me to do over there," I shouted up the stairs. "Maybe keep the return flight flexible?"

His response was so measured and obliging, I wondered if he was demonstrating how his unconditional love extended to helping me carve my dreams into reality. Alternatively, and more understandable in the circumstances, there was every chance he was welcoming the opportunity to have a break from me.

As days melted into weeks, my excitement simmered like lava. There was so much I wanted to see and do in the insomniac city. Not that I'd sunk so low as to call it a bucket list. No way was I about to tick off the Empire State Building and Central Park like items on a funereal shopping list. And I had no ambition to "do" New York, either. In fact, the only thing worse than bucket lists is people "doing places." I wanted to surrender to the city and let it claim me with its gritty vitality. New York was going to "do" me.

To anyone who would listen, I tried not to gush about my impending trip. The man-bunned barista at our neighborhood café beamed approval over my takeout latte. My good friend Greg was less impressed.

"What's happened, darling?" he said, disdain dripping through the phone line from London. "Are you having one of those brain hiccoughs people get at our age?"

Greg and I first met in the dress-up corner back in preschool. Even then I trusted his judgment. He persuaded me the milkmaid's outfit suited me to a tee, which freed up the fairy queen's gown for him.

"But it's the world's greatest city."

"That's just a logo New Yorkers invented to make themselves feel better about living in the world's worst hell hole," he said. "Stay away from those yellow taxis, whatever you do. The drivers murder people."

The vehemence of his reaction was unexpected.

"You're not jealous, are you?" I asked.

"How could I be? I'd much rather stay in a place where the beggars don't carry guns."

"New York beggars are armed?"

"Anyway, what are you doing leaving that gorgeous husband of yours?"

Greg had always been besotted with Philip.

"Do I smell a hint of divorce?" he added hopefully.

I didn't have answers to either of his questions. All I knew was my knee was sore and my neck ached. Since the kids had left home it wasn't as if I needed to hang around for them.

Son Rob and his wife Chantelle were up to their armpits in house renovations, their jobs, and their adorable daughters. My granny guilt meter went off the scale imagining Grandparents Day at Annie and Stella's preschool and the empty seat where I should be. All the other grannies who'd hobbled along on their walkers would refrain from asking where I was in case I'd taken a shortcut to the cemetery. Our younger daughter Kath was immune to my activities. She was off to college and in a parallel universe that involved dressing up as an elf and fighting Orcs in a park near the university. There was only one more person to break the news to.

Our older daughter, Lydia, seemed surprised the afternoon I called to suggest we take a walk in Victoria Gardens, the dog park just down the road from our place.

As we watched a man toss a ball for an arthritic Alsatian, I fought the urge to tell her how much prettier she looked since she'd stopped shaving her head, and how happy I was she'd become a secular Buddhist and braved a speed dating night to acquire a boyfriend. Living in a shared house with hipsters clearly suited her.

"How's Ramon?" I asked.

She emitted a dry cough. Only a mother would notice the way her hands were forming the shape of fists at her side. She didn't need to be defensive. I was hardly going to suggest we roll out a picnic rug and google bridal gowns. That said I liked Ramon immensely. Half Sri Lankan and raised Catholic, he had a whimsical sense of humor that was an ideal foil to her serious nature.

"Fine," she said, watching a skateboarder trundle toward the gates in the distance.

We were both bruised from our harrowing battles around the time of my breast cancer. I'd been hurt and furious when she'd taken off to Sri Lanka to become a Buddhist nun instead of staying home to provide emotional support through the mastectomy. In turn, she'd been perplexed and affronted by my lack of understanding of her need for spiritual growth.

Though our relationship had improved since she'd returned to Australia to complete her psychology studies, we still tended to circle each other like cats in a basement.

We found a bench under a tree and settled in the leafy shade.

"I'm going to New York." The statement sounded clumsy, and oddly shocking.

A golden retriever galloped in front of us, its tongue waving like a dishcloth. A bird trilled the opening notes of a jazz number. Lydia remained silent.

"I know, you think I'm crazy wanting to go there, you must think it's a dump, but . . ." I searched for the right words. "I really want to see *The Book of Mormon*. You know, the musical about the Mormon boys sent to convert people in Uganda. It's hilarious."

What was I saying? Lydia hated musicals. Besides, through her years of hard-core Buddhism she'd been forbidden to step inside a theater, which had been no hardship in her case.

"Are you serious?" she asked in a tone that implied I might need professional help.

"It's won a raft of Tonys," I said. "It'll be years before they bring it to Australia. I got the CD off Amazon. Have you heard 'Spooky Mormon Hell Dream'?"

"No, are you *really* going to New York?" she asked, fixing me with the psychologist expression that sears into my soul and makes it impossible to lie.

"Well, yes. My publishers think it's a good idea, with the new book coming out."

One of the curses of being a writer's daughter is you're destined to end up in print. I still wasn't sure how Lydia felt about me portraying our dramas in *Cats & Daughters*. Months earlier, watching her solemn expression as she'd read through the manuscript, I'd half expected her to hurl it on the floor and forbid me to send it to the publisher. Instead, she'd been incredibly forgiving and generous.

"How long for?" she asked, her face turned away, her tawny hair gleaming in the dappled light.

Why did everyone keep asking that?

"I haven't decided."

I knew what she was thinking. New York, of all places. Center of global capitalism, crass materialism, and everything nonspiritual. A fox terrier galloped through the gates and snapped at the heels of the old Alsatian.

"Why don't you come along?" I asked to fill the silence.

Lydia turned her face toward me. Her cheeks were pinker than usual. "I'd love to!" she said.

"Really?!"

My eyes filled with moisture. After everything we'd been through Lydia was volunteering to spend time with me in an environment hostile to her entire belief system.

"I couldn't stay for long . . ." she said.

*Yeah, right,* I thought. She's having second thoughts and wriggling out of it.

"But I could be there for maybe ten days at the beginning of your trip," she added.

She could have knocked me over with an incense stick.

## Chapter Three

# FOSTERING A KITTEN—NOT

*A cat never likes to be cornered.*

The only thing better than the idea of spending open-ended time in New York was the thought of having Lydia all to myself there for ten days. Voluntarily at that. If I didn't invade her space or say too many tactless things, there was a chance we'd come to forgive each other's differences and like each other again. With her by my side, the city wouldn't be so overwhelming. Settling into a new life of freedom would be much easier with her there ready to catch me if my knee gave out.

To my delight, she offered to scour the net for an Airbnb apartment.

Michaela told us to avoid Morningside Heights, the Columbia University district and anything above 96th Street. She suggested we find a safe, convenient apartment near hers in Chelsea. We were disappointed when Lydia's search of that area proved fruitless. Noho and Soho were also no goes, along with the Highline and the Flatiron districts. However, she managed to unearth two possibilities in the West Village. I sent the addresses off to Michaela and waited for her advice.

Next morning, I leapt out of bed and raced Jonah to the computer.

Jonah tap-danced across the keyboard while I tried to decipher the email.

> Hi Helen, I don't think you've met our marketing director, Vida Engstrand, but she's also a great cat lover. Just the other day we were talking about the tragic number of animals that were left homeless after Hurricane Sandy—and we've come up with what we hope you'll think is a brilliant idea . . .

Jonah's tail swished across the screen to block my view. I grabbed him and plonked him on my lap.

> How would you feel about fostering a shelter kitten while you're in New York?

My throat tightened. Had Michaela and Vida been out drinking?

> While you're having fun and frolics with your American bundle of fur, you'd also be helping our community. What do you think?

A kitten?! They couldn't know one of the reasons I was going to New York was to take a break from sleeping under a feline. Even if they did, I had no idea why they imagined I'd want to mop up puddles when I could be swanning around the Met.

Jonah emitted a regal yowl and blinked up at me as if to say, "They've got you now!"

Reading the email for the third time, I watched a glorious new phase of freedom in the world's greatest city shrink to an endless round of shoveling kitty litter.

"What's the matter?" Philip called from the kitchen.

My wail of despair must've echoed down the hall. He appeared, tea in hand, at my study door.

"Is that a new thing?" he asked when I told him. "Going to some other country and fostering an animal while you're there?"

Jonah bounced off my lap onto my shoulders and adopted the boa constrictor hold around my neck.

"No, it's not and I'm not about to start a new craze," I said, unraveling Jonah. "They're insane."

My husband, who has long since given up passing judgment on other people's mental conditions, slid into his suit jacket, kissed my forehead, and went to work.

There was only one person to turn to. I first met Olivia at a fundraiser for terminally ill children. With the heart of a saint and the mind of a diplomat, she has truckloads of style. When she isn't helping struggling artists, she's entertaining European royalty. Olivia's social skills are legendary. She could smooth out the Himalayas if she had to.

"Fostering a kitten in New York?!" she echoed. "Impossible! Anyway, what do you want to go *there* for? The only people ruder than Parisians are New Yorkers. You'll get mugged."

"But they're my publishers," I told her. "They'll think I'm a fraud if I turn them down."

I could hear Olivia's brain whirring at the other end of the line. Jonah flicked his tail across my nostrils while I repressed a sneeze.

"No need to panic," she said. "It's hard enough to find anywhere to stay in New York. You'll never find a place that's willing to take a kitten."

Olivia was always three steps ahead.

"Play along with them," she continued. "Give the impression you're looking for a pet-friendly accommodation. I promise you walls will grow whiskers before that happens."

"So, I'll be able to admit defeat with a clear conscience?"

"Absolutely."

"They won't hate me?"

"How could they?" she said. "It's a win–win."

Not for the first time, I was amazed by Olivia's brilliance. Her talents were wasted unraveling the complexities of my life when she could be running the UN. I put the phone down and googled "NYC Pet Friendly Apartments." As I scanned the results, a smile settled on my lips. There were more motels on Mars than cat-friendly apartments in New York.

After emailing Michaela to say I'd be delighted to foster a kitten, I went out and treated myself to a double strength latte with biscotti dipped in white chocolate icing. It felt good to be in charge of my own life again.

Next morning, the computer screen lit up with another message from Michaela.

> Dear Helen, Are you ready for "your" American kitten? I got an enthusiastic response from Bideawee, which is one of our local shelters with an excellent reputation.

Her enthusiasm was terrifying. I showed the email to Lydia, who'd dropped by to borrow a tent from the attic. She and Ramon were off camping for the weekend.

"I'm not doing it," I said.

Lydia seemed intrigued.

"But kittens are so cuddly," she said, gathering Jonah off my lap and sinking her nose in his neck.

"I know, but remember what a nightmare this one was when he was little." Baby Jonah had landed in our household with the subtlety of a hydrogen bomb that week after my mastectomy. But he'd also contributed much-needed laughter and warmth at a gloomy time.

"I'll help look after it."

My daughter's maternal instincts were in overdrive.

"Thanks, but I've done some research and it's a hopeless cause. There aren't any pet friendly apartments in New York."

Lydia ran her hand over Jonah's long, silky spine.

"Would you mind if I take a look on the net?" she asked.

It was a harmless enough request.

After a while, I started to enjoy pretending to be a cat foster mother applicant. No doubt con men revel in similar highs of wickedness mingled with a dread of being caught.

Vida reported that Bideawee had a temporary shortage of kittens. They were hoping the few they had would be adopted out by Easter time. When she asked if I'd be willing to take an adult cat, I felt a pang of disappointment as a vision of a round-eyed cuddle bundle faded to a streetwise tabby. Which was ridiculous, considering I had no intention of fostering anything larger than a dust mite. Lying through my fingertips, I told her an adult cat would be even better than a kitten, though (remembering Jonah's spraying habit and assuming an adult shelter cat would have issues around rejection) I would prefer a female.

A few days later, Vida sent an email saying the shelter would like to do a background check. I was flattered they thought I had a past that could be remotely complicated. And of course, it was good that they wouldn't lend a feline to just anyone. I was enormously impressed by the thought and care Bideawee and my publishers were putting into this doomed fostering project. After that, there was a reassuring silence.

It was broken several days later by a message from Vida.

Hi Helen,

I hope you're well. Bideawee says they have a few cats in mind, but they're hoping they'll be adopted out before April.

They want to know if you'd be open to fostering an adult cat with special needs? They have a few FIV+ cats that are in a special ward. They're very sociable and sweet, but would need a foster home without any cats.

You'd need to meet the adoption center manager a few days before you pick up the cat to go over what the care would entail and sign foster forms.

What are your thoughts? Are you okay with taking on a special needs cat?

Many thanks,

Vida

Panic stricken, I called Olivia.

"A cat with *AIDS?*" she said. "How New York 1980s can they get?"

"It's not transferrable to humans," I said.

Olivia thought I should put my foot down, but I said yes. If they'd asked me to adopt a three-legged Bengali tiger with syphilis I'd have said bring it on.

Because it was *never going to happen.*

There was one thing I had not counted on, however. Lydia is a Taurus born in the year of the ox in the hour of the ox. Once she's decided to do something, she digs her hooves in and refuses to give up. The best way to get her to make something happen is to tell her it's impossible.

After spending a weekend online, she appeared glowing at our front door. "Look at this!" she said, opening her laptop on the kitchen table.

I sat down and sifted through images of a small but livable-looking studio apartment. Hardly the Sofitel, but it wasn't a tent, either. The most attractive photo featured a black, almost certainly vinyl sofa sitting on pine floorboards under a poster of the Flatiron Building.

"It's a great location in Midtown," she said. "Halfway between the UN Building and Grand Central."

It sounded like a theme song, but then everything does in New York.

The price was reasonable and it was miraculously available for the month of April.

"And here's the best part," Lydia said, pointing out a line of fine print under the photo. I lifted the laptop off the table and peered at the tiny writing. A rock formed in my chest as two words came into focus: "Pet Friendly."

*"Really?"* I said. "That can't be right. I can't see any scratching posts in this photo."

Lydia fixed me with her psychologist look.

"You're just going to have to man up about this fostering thing," she said.

## Chapter Four

# LOVE IN THE GAPS

*A feline is always ready to sniff out a new neighborhood.*

Nobody is neutral about New York. They will tell you it's a cesspool or the most fantastic place on Earth. Whatever their opinion, they will never ask why you are going. It's understood a person has not fully lived until they have been.

I pressed my face against the side window as our cab merged with traffic streaming into Manhattan. Glittering needles of skyscrapers pierced the last blush of sunset. Confident of their beauty, they twinkled at us, knowing we'd soon be joining the millions addicted to living in and around them. Lydia sat in silence in the backseat as I pointed out the Empire State Building.

"See?" I said, jabbing my finger against the glass. "To think it was the tallest building in the world for nearly forty years."

With a jolt of horror, I realized Mum used to do the same thing, hammering her index finger against car windows to draw our attention to the latest architectural styles in milking sheds. Any danger of morphing into my mother had gone. I had become her.

My desperation for Lydia to love the city was matched only by my hope she might understand and warm to me a little over the next ten days.

It wasn't anyone's fault our personalities were close to opposite ends of the spectrum. Like the finger jabbing, it was gene stuff. If I could give up my tendency to lecture, there was a chance she might stop retreating into the monastic cell inside her head.

At 28, the poor girl had an entire youth to catch up on. Over the next ten days I planned to immerse her in everything she had turned her back on through five years of religious devotion—theater, galleries, and shopping for clothes other than sandals and robes. There would be plenty of time for book promoting after she had returned to Australia. Who knows what I'd get up to after she had left?

She had spent so long meditating in Asian temples, I was nervous she might disapprove of my infatuation with a place where Western culture reaches its logical conclusion. As we rattled into Manhattan, I took her silence for awe. Not even a nun could turn up her nose at a city exuding so much glitz.

It seemed an opportune moment to tell her about Michaela's ice dancing party. I somehow hadn't found the right moment to mention it before.

"Her *what?*" Lydia turned to face me.

"You know," I said, faking confidence. "Ice dancing party. New Yorkers have them all the time. I didn't think you'd be interested."

"Michaela takes *ice?*"

"Of course not. It's ice skating . . . I think."

"Does that mean we have to dance on ice, too?"

I didn't think so.

"We'll be pretty tired," I said, thinking whatever people did at an ice dancing party, it would be throwing her in the deep end. "You don't have to come along if you don't want to."

To my surprise, she said she did.

Our Airbnb host, Ted, had told us our apartment wasn't going to be ready till the next day, so we'd booked a place to stay overnight near Times Square. Darkness had fallen by the time the cab turned onto a narrow street and glided to a halt outside a shabby, dimly lit building. I scanned the entrance for a sign indicating it was an actual hotel.

"Is this it?" I asked.

"It sure as hell ain't *that!*" the driver said, shrugging at a skeleton of scaffolding propping up a building on the other side of the street.

Nothing goes wrong when I travel with Philip. I trail after him like a child through airports and hotel lobbies. Tickets and passports appear in a flash from the plastic wallet he carries inside his breast pocket. Suitcases disappear off conveyor belts to manifest mysteriously at my side. And hotels always look like hotels. I checked my phone. My latest text about taxicabs smelling the same all over the world had gone unanswered. He was probably on his way to work.

Night air sliced the back of my throat as Lydia and I scrambled out of the cab. New York's spring felt like the depths of an Australian winter. We grabbed our bags and ventured into what turned out to be a lobby. A rickety elevator carried us to the seventh floor, where I shunted the plastic key in the lock of room 74. The door drifted open to reveal a compact double bed encased in a 1980s style floral quilt.

Stale air tickled my nostrils, but Lydia was unperturbed. She assured me that compared to sleeping on the monastery floor, sharing a bed with me would be luxury. Besides, she added, people who are really tired sleep anywhere. I had a vision of shivering in a sleeping bag next to Philip in a tent perched on the edge of a precipice in New Zealand's high country. (It was early in our courtship when I was trying to convince him I loved camping as much as he did.) After a day trudging through wet bush I was exhausted, but sleep was impossible due to the presence of a large, furry animal snorting at the tent flap.

I picked up the avocado green phone from the bedside table. A weary voice at the other end of the line said the hotel was fully booked. There was no possibility of us moving to a room with two single beds, ma'am.

The receptionist said "ma'am" in a tone that implied it wasn't a compliment.

Lydia disappeared into the bathroom. Going by my watch (which was still on Australian time) it would still be morning back in Melbourne. If Philip wasn't out jogging, he'd be feeding Jonah the first of the 124 bags of diced chicken I'd left in a mosaic pattern in the bottom of the freezer. With luck, he would have remembered to transfer one of the little bags to the main part of the fridge to defrost overnight. More likely, he was dropping lumps of frozen chicken in Jonah's bowl, leaving the cat to fight it out with the ants while it was defrosting.

I dug the phone out of my handbag and punched *Arrived safely. Love you xxx*. His text flashed back seconds later. The man was steady as a heartbeat.

I pulled my boots off and flopped on the bed. The mattress wobbled resentfully. It was a relief to stretch out on a soft horizontal surface that wasn't hurtling through the air at unfathomable speed. As I dropped into a deep and welcome sleep, it occurred to me if I could order my own death, one like this would be acceptable. Painless, profound, peaceful . . .

A gentle hand shook my shoulder.

"Aren't we going to the ice party?" Lydia asked.

Jerking awake, I rolled off the bed and bolted

for the shower. Lydia passed me a towel through the door and asked if I knew where we were meeting Michaela.

"There must be a patch of ice somewhere in this town," I said, pumping a bottle claiming to be shampoo and body wash all in one. "I wrote it down on the back of the yellow paper with the addresses on it. She's having it downstairs somewhere. Sounds like a warehouse basement."

While I perched on the edge of the bed and toweled my hair into unruly spikes, Lydia asked what people did at ice dancing parties. She might as well have been seeking etiquette guidance to a fertility ceremony in New Guinea.

We unzipped our bags and pulled out our warmest clothes. What had I been thinking packing a short-sleeved shirt covered in pine-apples? I squeezed back into my boots, which had gone down a size since we left Melbourne.

There was no doubt my brain was on a jet lag merry-go-round. Since waking from the grave five minutes earlier, it was now craving coffee and adventure.

I decided watching a bunch of crazy New Yorkers ice dance would be the perfect opportunity for us to wear my hand-knitted ski caps. Before we left Australia, I'd been through another manic ski cap phase, knitting one for every person I love.

I hoped they would appreciate the devotion that

went into each ski cap. In every row of stitches are gaps that are neither wool nor open air. Into those spaces silvery parts of myself were spun to protect and nurture the recipient.

With each year, I become more aware of the power in spaces around things. There is truth and magic in those gaps. I learn more about a person by examining the energy they exude than the words they say, or even their facial expressions. This must be how animals observe the world. No doubt our baby selves had the ability, too, until we succumbed to a world fraught with anxiety and mind-numbing technology. It's in the spaces of so-called nothingness I'm able to connect with loved ones who have gone, to discover they're always with me.

Anyway, it turned out not everyone I care about wanted to look like a homicidal sheep shearer. Besides, even I had to admit the mohair wool in some of my creations was scratchy. My list of potential ski cap recipients was downgraded to anyone who'd have one.

If nothing else, my ski caps were warm. I took a yellow one from my suitcase and tossed it at Lydia. It disappeared discreetly inside her coat pocket. She slid a flimsy headband from her backpack.

"You'll freeze your ears off in that thing," I said pulling my red ski cap over my ears. The effect was more hillbilly than hipster.

According to Michaela's instructions, the ice rink was a ten-minute walk away. We went downstairs and were momentarily dumbstruck by the sea of humanity surging along the sidewalk outside. The pre-theater crowd, I guessed. Or maybe they were on their way to Times Square to do whatever people did there. Faces were bright and expectant as we heard excitement articulated in a dozen different tongues. Asian, European, young, or semi-decrepit, they were all bonded by the knowledge that tonight they were honorary citizens of the most vibrant city on Earth. Lydia and I dived into the tide, our breath forming white puffs in front of us.

As I accelerated to keep pace with the crowd, my worn-out labels seemed to peel away. Mother, grandmother, writer, and errant wife meant next to nothing in this swell. I was simply one human among millions, a single cell in a giant organism. It was exhilarating.

## Chapter Five

# AN INSPIRING GLIDE

*A cat is more a mystery to unravel*
*than a problem to be solved.*

Trailing after Lydia down West 47th Street was giving me plenty of time to admire the back of her brown bob. Young people have no idea how lustrous their hair is, and how fleeting that glossy growth.

As we filed past gleaming storefronts, I was grateful she was showing no signs of irritation at having to slow down for me.

If she'd paused for a second, I'd have caught up and pointed out a glorious mural set in stone. Art Deco's glamorous modernity took the planet by storm in that gush of optimism between the world wars. Though the style originated in France, New York is its spiritual home with the Chrysler Building as its high temple.

"Can't be far now," she said over her shoulder.

We turned a corner to confront an impressive row of national flags drooping from their poles. Above them, vertical lines of a building soared seventy stories into the night.

"Rockefeller Center," I said to Lydia, who had stopped to admire the sight.

But she wasn't listening. She was staring down at the plaza below us—and the most famous ice rink in the world.

There was no mistaking the gilded statue of Prometheus. The classically proportioned beauty has starred in countless movies, usually under the giant Christmas tree, where couples discover their love is true after all.

Prometheus has been soaring almost horizontal in languorous majesty since 1934. In an impressive balancing act, he holds a clump of fire in his right hand while keeping a shawl draped over his man parts.

I looked down at the glistening rectangle of ice. Apart from a lonely Zamboni machine leaving a silvery trail in its wake, the rink was empty. Maybe we'd missed the show.

We went downstairs where a female guard ushered us through a gate beside the rink. A small group of people was huddled in the semidarkness. It was hard to make out facial features but at least half were older males, and they seemed welcoming. There was no sign of Michaela.

A man greeted us in the gentlemanly lilt of *Gone with the Wind*. Carrying a video camera in one gloved hand, he took my hand in the other and introduced himself as Gene. Our words emerged in a series of icy clouds that hovered in the night air as if they were reluctant to leave.

With relief I noticed Gene was wearing something that could pass as a ski cap, except it was considerably more finely woven and elegantly shaped than mine. Lydia pulled her collar up and tugged the headband over her ears.

"You're just in time for Michaela's solo," he said.

*Solo?*

The ice took on a magical glow. Strains of Tchaikovsky struck up from an invisible source. Crowds gathered around the upper level of the plaza and peered over the rails.

As the music reached a crescendo, a woman spun onto the ice. She was wearing a crimson cloak and traditional Russian headgear worthy of a czarina. But it wasn't Michaela. She was taller, more statuesque. As she smiled at the audience and spread her arms, her cloak parted to reveal a short, gold-trimmed dress.

The woman was probably older than me and had been dealt a similar genetic build. Yet she wasn't hiding in loose knits in front of afternoon game shows. Watching her keep pace with the music in bold, rhythmical strides, I marveled at her grace and fitness. I tried to imagine myself inhabiting her body, how it felt to glide across the ice in full makeup, smiling and confident I wasn't going to tumble in a humiliating heap. My right knee began to ache in sympathy.

Our group applauded as she completed a leisurely spin, bowed, and left the rink.

When the music stopped, a sprite in dainty white boots sailed onto the ice. Her pastel pink dress hung in folds from her waist and finished just above her knees. Streamers fluttered from her sleeves. With her petite figure and curly blond hair framed against Prometheus's gold, she seemed to have sprung from another world.

"That's Michaela!" I whispered, thudding Lydia's jacket with my elbow.

Our group waited in respectful silence. Gene raised his camera as she floated through her routine like a bird riding a thermal wave.

The evening concluded with a group performance, faultless to the last twirl. We cheered from the sidelines alongside the women's adoring male partners. Nobody in the group was under 40, yet the couples flung their arms around each other in what seemed genuine passion. Maybe the city's water supply was laced with hormones. Whatever their secret, these women and their mates were demonstrating that the second half of life could be an inspiring glide.

Michaela stepped toward us, her coat belted up over her costume. With her glowing skin and zircon eyes, there was a hint of Marilyn Monroe about her. But anyone who mistook Michaela for a ditzy blonde would be in for a shock. I'd seen her dissect a manuscript with the coolheaded accuracy of a microsurgeon.

As we followed her and the group to a nearby bar, I felt the rest of my life was settled. I'd move to New York City and sign up for JoJo's Cool Workout Class on Ice. Though JoJo Starbuck is an Olympic medalist, she instructs at all levels. When her students aren't being ice princesses, they're at day jobs in real estate, finance, law, and other professions. I'd soon learn to ignore the curious onlookers leaning over the rails under the flags, and sail across the rink with the ice dancer's beatific smile.

My silhouette would take on the well-honed shape of a statue as I perfected the art of skating backward, spirals, hops, and maybe even jumps.

Over a glass of wine, Michaela described how she and her friends met at the skate house three or four mornings a week at 7 a.m., weather permitting. They'd help themselves to coffee and continental breakfast before starting their warm-up exercises.

In December before practice, they stopped and talked to the animal handlers walking the animals who live in Radio City Music Hall during the *Christmas Spectacular*. Sometimes, they were even invited to pet the camels because, as expected, New York City dromedaries were well mannered and clean.

In January, it was still dark when the class met. Little white lights sparkled in the trees around the plaza. As the sun rose over Saks Fifth Avenue, JoJo helped her students improve their skills and move their skating fantasies a bit closer to reality.

I couldn't wait to get started. All I needed

was skates and a $350 season ticket giving me unlimited time at the rink and a locker.

I'd only been there a few hours, but the vibrancy of the place was making me feel like a kid again.

Mingling with amiable strangers in the warmth of the bar, I watched crimson wine tumble into my glass. It was as if these people had been expecting me, and I was finally home. Lydia seemed happy, too. A striking blonde woman introduced herself as Karen Auerbach, the publicity director. She took Lydia aside to fill her in on the intricacies of the New York publishing scene.

It was an author's dream to have Vida, Michaela, Karen and their team going to so much trouble arranging a raft of interviews and a special cat store event. Though grateful for their efforts, I was nervous how *Cats & Daughters* was going to be received in the United States. No doubt they were hoping to replicate the success of *Cleo*.

Anyone who thinks a writer is solely responsible for a publishing hit is clawing at the wrong scratching post. As far as I know, nobody sits at a window with a view over rolling hills and channels a best seller into the stores (most professional writers I've met have desks facing blank walls, anyway).

Some kind of magic has to happen to inspire a chain of talented people to invest their skill and enthusiasm in the project. From agents and editors to publicists, bookstore owners, and reviewers, a book passes through countless hands before it reaches the most important person of all—the reader. In all honesty, *Cleo* had been a glorious combination of luck and timing. A fluke. I was just a scribbler from the other side of the planet with a tendency to bump into furniture.

My phone vibrated against my hip inside my pocket.

> **Gr8 u have arrived safely. I've given Jonah his pill. On my way to work xxx.**

It was such a *measured* message, so trusting and straightforward, I felt momentarily guilty. Still, if I was home right now, I'd be bent in front of the washing machine sorting whites from coloreds.

Though I raised the glass there was no need for alcohol. I was already intoxicated, drunk on New York. A slender woman with long hair moved toward us with the grace of a tiger. Her bright smile and dark eyes seemed familiar.

"Here's to your foster cat!" Vida said, clinking her glass against mine.

*Oh. The cat.* I'd hoped they'd given up on that harebrained scheme. But no, Vida said she'd been in touch with the shelter and they were expecting us on Monday. When I explained we'd barely have time to settle into our apartment by then, Vida and Michaela looked crestfallen, as if a homeless cat was enduring hours of suffering because of my delay tactics.

I took a swig of wine and said Monday would be fine. Michaela's face lit up like Times Square. She said she'd visit as soon as the cat had settled in.

Back in our hotel room two hours later, I was so tired I brushed my teeth with face cream.

When I was finally tucked into bed, I thought of Vida toasting our future foster cat. The only way I could survive the insane plan would be with a low maintenance animal.

Greg was always telling me about the power of visualization. Closing my eyes, I conjured up an image of a hefty tortoiseshell. A sedate female with a name like Mavis, my foster cat would have been recently orphaned after 18 years with her widowed librarian owner. Mavis's interest in human contact would be limited to watching me spoon fish flakes onto a saucer. She would pass her days dozing on a window ledge while Lydia and I went on shopping safari in Saks Fifth Avenue. Unlike Jonah, Mavis would hardly notice when we arrived home, on account of deafness. She'd acknowledge our presence with an offhand flick of her tail. Mavis wouldn't be unfriendly or destructive, just healthy, quiet, clean, and sane. I slipped into a milky bowl of Mavis dreams.

## Chapter Six

# SEX, DRUGS, AND JUNK FOOD

### Palace or drain—
### a cat can live anywhere.

A roar of industrial strength drilling jolted me awake. I sprang out of bed and pulled the curtains open. Lydia was quickly at my side. It was dark outside, but across the street an insomniac demolition crew was already at work. With our walls and windows vibrating, trying to get back to sleep was pointless. Besides, I wanted to introduce Lydia to her first diner.

"You want *what?!*" the world-weary waitress shouted.

"Two lattes, please."

She shoved her pencil in her pocket and slouched back to the kitchen. A pasty-face waiter trudged toward us and asked us to repeat our order.

"We don't do no lattes," he said.

"How about cappuccinos?"

Exasperated, he threw up his hands.

"No fancy espresso machine here, lady!"

The waitress returned to fill our cups with fluid that could have been diverted from a nearby drain.

"Don't worry," I said to Lydia. "This stuff will taste like nectar after we've been here a few days."

Lydia smiled down at her pancakes spread

like a pair of tropical islands over her plate. She trickled a swirl of maple syrup over the top. I was momentarily embarrassed when my mountain of scrambled eggs and grilled potatoes arrived gasping for breath under a pile of bright pink bacon. A quick glance at other tables assured me the waitress hadn't put the kitchen on giantess alert. The man next to us was working through three porterhouse steaks and an Everest of french fries.

We sluiced down glasses of neon orange juice with iced water. No matter how frigid the weather, every self-respecting diner serves water clinking with ice cubes.

The waitress slapped a couple of plates of buttered toast on the table in case we were still feeling peckish. I could tell Lydia was beginning to warm to New York.

"Is this *normal?*" she whispered across the table.

"Totally."

"How come I've seen so many skinny people?"

"There's room for every quirk in this town," I said. "If we had a thing for collecting Icelandic moose dung, there'd be at least twenty other people on Manhattan with the same obsession."

"You mean there's a moose dung society?"

"Probably. Heaps of people go to downtown diners, but on the Upper East Side thousands survive on nothing but air and quinoa."

Lydia hadn't touched her second pancake. I couldn't look at my potatoes. We shoved the plates aside and headed out into the street.

In my best *Sex and the City* imitation, I raised an arm, but the cabs buzzed past like hornets on a mission. The mature woman's invisibility cloak at work again. After about twenty minutes, Lydia spotted a cab with its light on. She raised her arm and lunged forward, leaving the driver a choice of running her over and spending months in court, or hitting the brakes and letting us climb in.

Sitting in the backseat, keys safely tucked in my pocket, I squeezed her hand as we swerved past Central Park toward our new home. She was proving herself a natural New Yorker. Locals talk down the fact they live in a mega metropolis. They say it's just a string of villages called neighborhoods. Everyone raves about their neighborhood. I couldn't wait to see ours. With it being so close to the UN, I imagined it awash with Daniel Craig lookalikes carrying poison dart umbrellas.

When the cab pulled up outside a world-worn pizza joint near the corner of East 44th Street, I was taken aback. The one-way thoroughfare that carved a short, businesslike line from the East River wasn't quite the blossom-lined boulevard I'd pictured.

We dumped our bags on the sidewalk. A North

African man wearing an ankle-length caftan and traditional cap was selling handbags from a stand near the corner. When we approached and asked directions, he pointed at a modest redbrick building sandwiched between two tall gray ones. Roughly six stories high and close to a century old, it gazed onto the street through unadorned windows, like an old lady who couldn't remember how she'd ended up in such frenetic surroundings.

A set of worn, narrow steps ran up to a front door painted a raucous scarlet. I climbed the steps, fumbled for the keys in my handbag, and issued a silent prayer to the God of Airbnb. *(Even if Ted doesn't exist and this whole thing is a scam, please let us in and give us a roof over our heads tonight.)*

Though the brass lock was scratched, it was shaped like a heart. It was the building's way of telling us that no matter how tired it looked from the outside, it still had soul. When the key turned smoothly and the door glided open, I felt weak with gratitude.

The front door creaked open to reveal a tiny hallway leading to a flight of steep, paint-spattered stairs. Dust particles drifted in beams of watery light. A background odor implied things had been living and dying between these walls for a very long time.

Our apartment was on the fourth floor, meaning

we'd have to climb "only" three sets of stairs, which I'd decided would be kill-or-cure therapy for my knee. The first challenge was going to be getting my coffin-sized suitcase up to our eyrie. Lydia offered to help haul my luggage up, but I didn't want her thinking she'd been invited along as a geriatric nurse. The suitcase was outrageously heavy. After two flights of stairs, my lungs were stinging. I paused to catch my breath while pretending to admire the doors arranged in a horseshoe around the stairwell. They were all shades of dark brown and firmly shut, as if whoever lived behind them had no intention of letting the world in. Meanwhile, the ambient aroma had intensified to eau de rotting vegetables mixed with blue cheese and unwashed feet.

I beckoned to Lydia to go ahead and, once I'd decided the danger of heart attack had subsided, heaved the suitcase up the final set of stairs.

"I think this is it," she said, her face overcast with confusion.

The stench, which was now overpowering, was emanating from the partially opened door in front of her. A cacophony of banging and clattering was coming from inside. The apartment—*our* apartment—was occupied by an incontinent poltergeist.

*"Hellooo?"* I called in the tentative tone my aunt used when dropping in on unsuspecting relatives.

There was a brief silence, followed by shuffling and a morose sigh. My instinct was to shove Lydia forward to find out what was going on. Even ancient warlords knew confrontations tend to unfold with less tension when initiated by a fresh-faced page.

But pleasantries would take time. I was desperate to get my boots off and lay down somewhere—no matter how smelly. Besides, whoever was in there needed to know we'd paid a month's rent in advance.

I stepped tentatively over the threshold to face a postapocalyptic scene. Floorboards were littered with discarded food wrappers, polystyrene cartons, plastic bags, and empty water bottles. Next to the fireplace, a trash can lay on its side vomiting a tangle of half-eaten noodles. Under the window, an unmade bed spilled an eruption of sheets and blankets onto the floor.

The apartment was unrecognizable from the stylish photos we'd seen online. The only items that looked familiar were the purple curtains and a glass-topped coffee table. A black vinyl bench ("comfortable sofa bed") was buried under what appeared to be a pile of tattered and well-worn undergarments.

Away from the window at the other end of the room, and bent over a kitchen sink was the most worn-out, unhappiest African American woman I'd ever seen. When I approached and asked what was going on, she rolled her eyes and said, "Some people are just plain animals."

Well, it was a pet-friendly apartment—actually, going by the dimensions it was more of a room. Whoever had taken the photos we'd seen online must've been using the biggest fish eye since Moby Dick. I checked for evidence of cats and dogs, but this was a mess only feral humans could make. I'm not fussy, and I've seen some wild student apartments in my time, but this was a cesspool worthy of a medieval village. Forcing the window open, I tried to imagine how our predecessors had spent their time holed up in here for a month—sex, drugs, junk food, repeat.

The cleaning woman said she'd been working since 6 a.m. and was desperate to get back to her family to cook them an Easter Sunday meal. My annoyance melted to sympathy. I started to feel responsible for the previous tenants who'd left the place a garbage dump on the assumption someone who had no choice would clean up after them.

Lydia and I nudged our bags against a wall and unbuttoned our coats. I grabbed a broom and swished it around. Lydia gathered up a couple of bulging garbage bags and carried them to bins downstairs.

"What were they *doing* in here?" I said, approaching the rank-smelling bed. At a minimum, the sheets would have to be stripped off and taken to a laundry.

"Don't touch that!" the cleaning person shouted across the room.

"Really?" I said, lifting a corner of the quilt.

"*No!*" she said. "You don't want to look in there. Believe me."

Grateful as she seemed for our help, the cleaning person said she'd get through the job faster on her own. She told us to go for a walk for a couple of hours. We needed to buy bath towels and a blanket for Lydia, anyway. The sofa bed was equipped with sheets only. I was tempted to pick up fresh linen for us both, but the woman said not to bother. She'd make our beds up with clean sheets.

I negotiated her bucket and peered through the bathroom door. It was tiny, with fittings circa 1970, but serviceable. The hem of the shower curtain was caked in green mold.

Feeling useless and relieved not to be needed at the same time, I pulled on my coat and ski cap, gave the cleaning person what I hoped was a generous tip, and scampered downstairs with Lydia.

"That place is the perfect size—for a cat," I said, tugging my ski cap over my ears and trudging in what I imagined was the direction of Bloomingdale's.

I waited for Lydia to tell me that she'd come around to thinking the cat fostering idea was stupid. She'd suggest I call Michaela and Vida in the morning to explain the situation. They would understand, and cancel our appointment with the animal shelter. But she galloped ahead down the street.

"Hurry!" she called over her shoulder. "There's a Holi festival!"

"A what?"

"It's a Hindu thing," she shouted. "They're celebrating the triumph of good over evil."

In most relationships, there's a grown-up and a child. With Lydia and me, the chronological roles are reversed. She thinks before she says anything, whereas I blurt out opinions to regret later at leisure. When we're together, I rely on her to rein in my more outlandish behavior. If her eyes glaze and she becomes quieter than usual, it's a sign I've pushed the boundaries too far. Partly because of this dynamic, I hadn't witnessed her letting herself go since she was about three years old.

I accelerated into a clumsy jog, but then stopped in my tracks. I could hardly believe it. Piercing the sky barely two blocks away was the most exquisite piece of architecture in the entire world. The Chrysler Building with its glittering tiara symbolizes everything I adore about New York. I called out to introduce her to the delights of this needle-like confection rising from the intersection of 42nd Street and Lexington Avenue. It had been the tallest building in the world for eleven months until the Empire State Building eclipsed it in 1931. But my voice dissolved in a thrum of traffic.

When I caught up with her, she was standing at the entrance to a small park. Drums thumped to the strains of Indian music, bodies twirled, arms waved. Faces were happy—and every one of them, from babies to grandparents, was spattered with neon powder paint.

I took her elbow and suggested we leave them to it, but she was entranced. Ignoring me, she slipped out of my grasp and into the crowd. Alarmed, I lost sight of her. A few minutes later, I caught a glimpse of her, head thrown back and laughing, her right cheek vibrant blue. I dived in to rescue her—only to have my ski cap bombed bright yellow. The first hit felt like an assault; the second, a green blob on my forehead, was more like a kiss.

As the music drew us into a hypnotic spiral, we were soon putting ourselves in the firing lines of reds, purples, and oranges—begging to be hit.

Dancing around with crazy, paint-bombing Indians in the middle of New York was like being drunk without touching a drop of vodka. Outsiders in this giant city, we'd been accepted and daubed by a group of other outsiders, who somehow embraced me with joyous feelings of belonging. Laughing under a shower of orange, I forgot about the prospect of inhabiting a rat hole

for the next month or two. We
and my feet were pleasantly p
  Miraculously, my knee w
Western medicine has a
thought, gyrating my hips
didn't have a meniscus tear, just a
dancing. As I shook my hands in the an,
of perpetual anxieties began to fade. Wallet a
passport stolen—so what? Mugged and thrown in
the Hudson—well, I'd had a good life.

Lydia spread her arms in the air and laughed.
I'd never seen her so uninhibited. Maybe we
were more alike than I'd thought. The city was
having a strange effect on us both. I could see
my husband's face at the sight of me covered
in splotches like a Jackson Pollock painting.
The stuff didn't seem to rub off, either. If I
could ever persuade him to move here there'd
be compromises, of course. We'd have to find a
neighborhood where they don't throw paint.

"We'd better get to the shops before they
close," Lydia said, appearing at my side. She was
back to her sensible self—apart from the fact she
was bright blue and green.

Two blocks along, the atmosphere changed
radically. Almost every face was white and
conservatively dressed. Horns stopped honking
and there were no more vividly speckled soul
mates to wave at. We seemed to have moved out
of the paint-throwing neighborhood to a part of

e people had never even *heard* of the
val. My red ski cap and I were now
yellow. I caught my reflection in a shop
w to see a hallucinogenic Big Bird.

e stumbled across a housewares store, where
young staff members looked too tired to jump
o conclusions. As we paid for our towels (blue),
Lydia's blanket (fake fur), and a shower curtain
(red and yellow stripes), the cashier didn't
seem to notice his customers resembled a pair
of brightly colored parrots. If he did, he wasn't
saying anything. This is New York, after all.

*Chapter Seven*

# A City with Heart

*There's no such thing
as just a cat.*

A set of purple curtains came into focus above my head as I woke from a hollow of sleep. Lydia was snoring gently under her fake fur blanket a few feet away. Poor kid. The so-called sofa bed was just a vinyl-covered plank, but she'd insisted it was comfortable. The room was chilly. Thank god we had bought the blanket for her. I pulled the covers up to my chin and tried to focus on the freshly laundered sheets rather than the bed's lingering aroma.

With most traces of the previous tenants gone, our new home revealed itself in all its glory. The only source of natural light was from the windows behind my bed. The front door and kitchenette at the other end of the room faded into shades of gloom.

The cleaning person had left a note saying she'd changed the code to the door lock. She'd scrawled the new numbers in bold pencil. Reassuring as it was, I was grateful for the additional row of bolts across the inside of the door.

It was a good thing Lydia was accustomed to sleeping in confined spaces. If she'd rolled over during the night, she would have landed on the glass coffee table. The vacant eye of a small television stared out at her from a few feet across the room.

A table just big enough for a chair and a laptop sat in the corner near my bed. Though I was aware a crippled Wi-Fi connection was a first world problem, I was relying on Skype to keep our long-distance marriage alive.

Cleared of rubbish and the worst of the smell, our studio took on a raffish charm. The fireplace next to the television hadn't been used for years from the look of it. Some enterprising soul had freshened it up with white paint and transformed it into what real estate agents call a period feature. Next to it, the daffodils we'd bought ourselves as a housewarming present the previous night glowed from a tall vase.

Even the smallest apartments have eccentricities. Next to the bathroom we discovered a large, airless room. The space was too cavernous to be called a closet, but it had a few wire coat hangers dangling from a pipe down the left-hand side. After we'd wheeled our suitcases in there we christened it the Bunker.

Rolling out of bed, I tugged the curtains and let out a cry of delight.

"What is it?" Lydia asked, bleary with sleep.

"There's a fire escape straight out of *West Side Story*!" I said. "Can't you just see Tony climbing up those steps and singing 'Tonight'?"

My daughter groaned and turned her face to the

wall. The act of forcibly not singing was making my sinuses throb.

Across the concreted building shaft, I made out the silhouettes of workers bent over their desks to start the day.

Though they were in another building, we were at the same level and they were just a few yards away. If one of them had looked up, they would have seen a wild woman in her nightie watching them.

I could see a tall man and a slightly built woman standing close to the window. They were engrossed in conversation and the tension between them was intimate enough to make me wonder if they were having an affair. But at second glance, his concentration was focused on her clipboard, not her cleavage.

Back in Melbourne, Philip would be climbing into his pajamas after a long day's work. Jonah would be waiting to pounce on our bed. I wondered how our feline was adjusting to having just one set of legs to snuggle into. I tried Skype again. After a series of watery bleeps, the line went dead. I told myself I wasn't missing them at all, just wondering how they were doing.

As I smoothed the bed covers and plumped the pillows, I hummed "America" (under my breath to avoid getting into trouble with my traveling companion). Our apartment was tiny and scruffy, but it was ours. I was already in love with it.

The only sobering thought was that in a few hours' time, unless I could think of a watertight excuse, we'd be sharing it with Mavis.

I stumped past Lydia to the bathroom. It had hardly enough room for a human toilet, let alone a litter box. As I rinsed the residue of yesterday's paint off my arms, I empathized with babies in the later months of pregnancy. My buttocks collided with the wall when I bent to pick up the soap. Our new shower curtain sucked at my thighs while water puddled on the floor. To be a New Yorker is to economize on movement.

After I'd dressed, thrown on some blush to hide residual paint blobs, and wandered into the kitchenette, Lydia asked if the animal shelter might be open yet.

"Hardly," I said, spooning ancient grains into a bowl.

"It's after nine."

"Yes, but we can't just go and collect a cat like that," I said, trying not to shatter a tooth.

"Why not?"

She listened like Judge Judy while I explained we'd need to acquire a litter box at least before we could think about letting a cat move in.

"No problem," she said, pulling on her long pants. "There's a pet supply shop across the street."

I urged her to slow down. She needed to shower and have breakfast. Then maybe we could squeeze in a visit to MoMA, and possibly even the Frick.

After she'd gulped down her antiquated grains, I followed her downstairs into a brilliantly crisp day. The handbag sellers were setting up their stall near the corner. Rows of vividly colored wares jostled in the breeze, competing for our attention.

"Wow! Aren't they adorable? Haven't you always wanted a bright yellow tote?"

Lydia stood back, tactfully ignoring my question.

"Or one with red polka dots!"

"Would it match any of your clothes?"

True, my wardrobe back home was full of frumpy tunics and sturdy shoes with minimal heels. And every handbag I'd ever owned was black. Anyone would think I belonged to a sect. All that was about to change.

"How about this gorgeous blue one?" I said, reaching to remove it from its hook so I could inspect the lining.

The salesman shot me an icy look. I lowered my hand, grabbed Lydia's arm and swept her around the corner.

"What's the matter?" she asked.

"He thought I was going to steal it!"

A homeless man sat hunched on a bench under a stainless steel sculpture. He held out his palm to a pair of executive types in long, dark coats. Locked in conversation, they strode past him down the hill toward the UN. This was the harsh, uncaring city Greg and Olivia had warned me about. Maybe I'd been foolish to imagine I could spend a month among people as cold as the concrete buildings they lived and worked in.

I knotted my scarf and grabbed Lydia's hand as we crossed the street. If we'd been tourists we'd have walked straight past the small, homey shop sandwiched between a Laundromat and a hardware store. An old ginger cat sat in the window and blinked at us. A bell tinkled as we pushed the door open to step into an Aladdin's cave of pet food and toys. While some of the brands were unfamiliar to us, the smell of meat mingled with sawdust was not. As we wandered down the aisle, the ginger cat padded after us with casual interest.

In a city made of sharp edges, the relief of seeing something so soft and linked to nature was beyond words. I wanted to gather him up in my arms and hug him.

"He must have been a tiger in a previous life," Lydia said.

"Well, hello mister," I said, turning and crouching on the floor. "You're a handsome fellow. What's your name?"

The cat twitched his whiskers and assessed whether I was worthy of his time.

"Bluebell," a gravelly voice said. "Her name's Bluebell. And she's a girl."

A woman gazed down at me through enormous round, purple spectacles. Her auburn hair was piled up in extravagant swirls. The accent had a Queens twang.

"Isn't it rare for a ginger cat to be female?" I asked, as Bluebell stepped forward to nudge my finger with her damp nose.

"Not rare," she said. "Unusual. Can I help you?"

Her tone was sharp, but the eyes behind the giant spectacles had a watery sadness. I began to wonder if she was one of those people whose life experiences have led them to prefer cats to humans.

"Well, yes I think you can," I said. "We're visiting from Australia."

"I thought so," she said.

"And we're going to foster a cat while we're here."

Her face melted in a smile, exposing two large front teeth with an endearing gap between them.

"That's a wonderful thing to do! What sort of cat are you getting?"

I found it heartwarming that two women from opposite sides of the globe could bond over a cat neither had met.

"We don't know yet, but probably a quiet old thing like your Bluebell."

"Bluebell's not old," the woman's tone was defensive. "She's only 14."

The shopkeeper needed Bluebell to hang around for a long time to come.

"You're right," I said, after a respectful silence. "Bluebell's practically a teenager. We had a cat who lived to 24."

"My Daffodil lived to 33," she said.

It's never a good idea to get into competitions about how long your cat survived.

"Did she?" I said. "That's amazing!"

"Daffodil was a he, not a she."

"Oh, I'm sorry. I thought . . ."

"Tulip, that's Daffodil's sister, was female. And so was Rose, their mother. But Daffodil and Magnolia were boys."

"Were they all ginger?" I asked taking a gray plastic litter box from the top of a pile.

"Mostly tabby," she said, following me to the cat food section. "They all lived a very long time."

The inherent sadness of owning a cat or dog is the knowledge they will leave too soon. When they do, the long-lived human is stricken with genuine grief. We can try to protect ourselves by not loving too much, but in the end it's impossible. For many, the grief after losing an animal equates the pain of mourning for a human friend or family member. Perhaps, it makes sense to adopt a tortoise or a parrot who might stand a chance of outliving us.

The range of cat foot was overwhelming.

Besides, I had no idea what our foster animal's preferences would be.

"We'll take this for now," I said lifting the plastic tray onto the counter.

"And please," the woman said, placing a bag of kitty litter on top of it. "I want you to have this as a gift."

"Really?"

The woman who had been so brittle a few moments ago had become softer than fur.

"It's a wonderful thing you're doing for New York," she said. "This is just a little thank-you. Come see me when you have your cat. If I'm not here, just ask for Doris. I won't be far away."

Numb with surprise, I thanked Doris and gave Bluebell one last pat before we left.

The hardware shop was a bewildering collection of kitchen implements and knickknacks. We made our way to the back of the store, where stacks of plates and mixing bowls towered over us.

"Are you looking for something?"

A young woman approached. The paleness of her skin was enhanced by a frame of lime green hair.

"Do you have any feeding bowls?" Lydia asked.

"For a person or a dog?"

New York humor can be deliciously blunt.

"A cat, actually."

The girl's face softened.

"I like cats," she said. "You're from England, aren't you?"

"We live in Australia, but we were both born in New Zealand," Lydia said.

"That's near Holland, isn't it?" the girl asked.

"Not really," I said. "It's where the Lord of the Rings comes from."

"So, let me get this straight," she said. "You guys are hobbits?"

We laughed and said we were, right to the toenails of our hairy feet.

"So how long have you been living in New York?"

It was natural for her to assume we had settled in. Why else would we have a cat? When Lydia explained we were on a fostering mission, the girl broke into a smile.

"Sophie!" she yelled. "Come over here! You gotta hear this."

A tall girl in an orange bandana appeared.

"These ladies come from the Lord of the Rings and they're fostering a New York cat," the green-haired girl explained. "They need a feeding bowl."

"That's amazing!" her friend said.

I could hardly believe how much a foster cat-to-be was changing people's attitudes toward us.

"We don't have a specific pet feeding bowl," the taller one said. "But wait. I've got an idea."

She dived behind a pile of cardboard boxes to retrieve a small red dish with silver fish etched into its surface.

"It's beautiful!" I said. "And perfect for a cat. How much is it?"

The young women exchanged looks.

"We want you to have it," the taller one said.

They were sweet girls, but I thought they needed to work on their communication skills.

"Yes, I know you'd like us to take it. But how much do I owe you?"

"Nothing," the younger one said. "Just have a great time with your cat."

Laden with our gifts, Lydia and I made our way back to the apartment in a daze.

"New Yorkers must have a real thing for their pets," Lydia said.

"Maybe it is because more than half the population lives alone," I said. "For a lot of people animals could be taking the place of significant others."

Either way, nothing could have prepared us for the generosity we had just experienced. I wished Greg and Olivia could have seen it.

If we'd been visiting New York as mere tourists, we'd never have met these kindhearted women and seen how quickly their crusty surfaces could dissolve.

Our rescue cat Mavis was working her magic.

## Chapter Eight

# A ROCK STAR IN FUR

*Caring for a cat is the first step towards self-healing.*

Lydia was revving like a Ferrari. As we made our way toward Bideawee on East 38th Street she bounded ahead. I called out to her so we could stop and admire the UN Building. Poised like a cigarette packet against the shimmering East River, it's the architectural equivalent of Don Draper. Though it has a sixties look, it was actually completed in 1952, proving itself yet another New Yorker ahead of its time.

Intrigued as I was to be visiting a big city animal shelter, I was wary of such places. When I was a kid, the animal pound was a dismal shed on the outskirts of town. A holding pen where unwanted creatures spent a few miserable days before being "humanely" destroyed, it reeked of death.

Besides, I was nervous about the cat. Even a placid one like Mavis might sense my reluctance and take it into her head to exact punishment.

"Is this it?" Lydia asked, stopping outside a modern, multistoried building smiling out across the river. The gleaming exterior couldn't have been further from my idea of an animal shelter. A small, ecstatic dog burst out of the doors. With its ears pricked and pink tongue flying, it pranced joyfully past us, as if a wonderful new life had just begun. When the man attached to his lead caught my eye his smile broadened.

"She's a fox terrier cross," he called over his shoulder, as the dog dragged him up the sidewalk. "We're calling her Gracie."

Inside, a warm and spacious lobby bustled with benign energy. A security guard stood discreetly by the door. There wasn't a hint of animal whiff about the place. Across the shining floor, a young couple sat holding hands. Their anxious faces reminded me of parents expecting their first child. When a woman appeared with a cat carrier in her arms, they looked up hopefully. Their smiles faded to disappointment as she walked straight past them into another room.

I could have spent the morning watching people meet their pets for the first time, but Lydia steered me toward a reception area. A smiling woman in her mid-thirties greeted us and introduced herself as Suzie. With her long ponytail and clear eyes, she beamed an almost angelic quality.

"We've been waiting for you," she said. "You're here for Bono, aren't you?"

The only Bono I knew about was a rock star with yellow glasses, and there'd probably be a lot more security if he was in the vicinity. I began to explain to her that whatever a Bono was, we weren't about to collect one.

"Jon's excited, too," she continued. "He's our cat assessment manager."

She whisked us into a small office, where a man sat bent over a desk. His oval face was framed with long dark hair. The softness in his eyes was overlaid with sorrow, or perhaps too much knowledge of what life can bring. His forearms were awash with ink. Tattooed people usually like to talk about their decorations, and I often use it as a conversation starter. But something held me back from bombarding him with cheap questions about the meaning of his art.

People who work with animals are often unusual, but I sensed something multidimensional about this man. Highly sensitive and attuned, he was a rare breed apart, a cat whisperer.

"This is the best thing that's ever happened to Bono," Jon Delillo said, smiling broadly.

The Bideawee people were lovely, but obviously misinformed. Clearing my throat, I repeated our story about coming from Australia to foster an ancient tortoiseshell.

Jon beckoned us to follow him across the foyer through two sets of doors into what amounted to an indoor cat jungle. A three-leveled scratching tree was entirely occupied by felines—a tabby, a ginger, and a pure white cat with eyes that were different shades of copper. I stepped over a large gray and white gentleman dozing on a mat in the middle of the room to say hello to a green-eyed calico crouched inside a carpet tunnel.

Then I saw her. Mavis—*our* Mavis waddling

toward a food bowl. Plump and barely able to move, the foster cat was about to enter my life.

"She's gorgeous!" I said, but nobody seemed to be listening. I figured the staff were so accustomed to people gushing over their wards they were deaf to fawning noises.

A few other cats slid into my peripheral vision. A couple of hefty felines similar to Mavis dozed on top of carpeted poles. Several more stared out from nooks. Two teenage tabbies curled together in a yin and yang circle.

A young woman sat in the corner with a lean tuxedo cat nestled in her lap. She introduced herself as Sadie, one of Bideawee's army of volunteers. Whatever its age, size, or color, every animal seemed content. Bideawee was clearly cat shelter heaven.

Though I liked Mavis, I was willing to be flexible. Really, any one of these noninteractive animals would be fine for us to foster. My reverie was interrupted when a black cannonball hurtled across the room. It propelled itself off the gray and white cat's belly and scrabbled up a scratching post to snare a fellow lodger's tail.

"You're gonna love Bono," Jon said.

"*That's* Bono?" I said, staring at the stream of confusion the creature had left in its wake. The other cats narrowed their eyes, hissed, and switched their tails as he bounced past.

I wasn't sure the creature even qualified as a

domestic cat. It looked more like a miniature lion. Apart from his oversized head, shaggy feet, and feather duster tip of his ridiculously long tail, he was entirely shaved.

I made a mental note to tell Greg to forget visualization. This primeval bundle of energy was nothing like Mavis. Watching Bono bounce across the floor, I couldn't decide if he was ugly or incredibly beautiful. With a flat, pushed-in face, he hardly seemed to have a nose.

"We're all crazy about him," Jon said. "You will be, too."

Jon could say what he liked, but I wasn't enthralled at the thought of having my New York freedom ruined by a hyped-up mini lion. A list of excuses was already forming inside my head. I could tell him I had an allergy to cats named after rock stars. Or that my ancient joints would crumble trying to keep up with a hyperactive maniac. Or that I could only consider taking on a vegan animal who identified as transgender.

"He's adorable!" Lydia cried, crouching on the floor and clicking her fingers at him. "Look at those eyes!"

From where I was standing I could only see the back of his fluffy mane. He put his head to one side and stepped tentatively toward her. She spoke softly to him and extended her hand to touch his forehead. At the moment of contact he bounced backward across the room as if she'd given him an electric shock.

"We had him shaved because his fur was matted," Jon explained, smiling fondly down at him.

When I asked how they'd managed to keep such a lively animal immobile long enough to be shaved, Jon admitted the grooming had been performed under a general anesthetic.

"Life's stressful for him being the smallest cat around here," Jon continued. "He has to spend around fifteen hours a day in a cage. The rest of the time he's constantly fighting to keep up with the others."

We watched the mini lion dodge occasional bats from larger cats as he pranced past their cages. Like big kids with a pesky baby brother, they had no qualms letting him know they were fed up with his boisterous ways. Squaring my shoulders, I started explaining this wasn't the sort of cat I had in mind. But deaf to my protest, Jon launched into a heartrending backstory.

Like thousands of other animals, Bono had lost his home during Hurricane Sandy when it had struck New York in October the previous year. After being found washed up and bedraggled on Long Island, he had been taken to a municipal shelter. Though Jon didn't elaborate, he gave the impression the cat's future would have been limited in that place. When I prodded him for more information, he said all he knew was that Bono had been abandoned or surrendered. Both words struck me as incredibly sad.

Because of Bono's friendly nature and beguiling combination of Persian and Maine coon, he was given a second chance. He was transferred to Bideawee in Manhattan, where he was more likely to find a permanent home. Jon reminded me Bono had been with them a full six months, which was a long time for any living creature to spend most of its days in a cage.

"But you said everyone loves him," I said. "Surely someone will adopt him?"

Jon shook his head.

"People are always drawn to him, but when they find out he has chronic kidney disease they back away."

A river boulder formed in my chest.

"Isn't that something old cats get?" I asked, watching Bono glide across the room. With his Ugg boots hardly touching the ground, he floated like a ballet dancer. That cat couldn't be dying. He was practically exploding with life.

"Not necessarily," Jon said, his mouth set in a grim line. "We think he's about four years old. That's usually a good age for adoption, but we understand why people don't want to take him. The treatment's expensive and it's going to end in heartache. Only a saint would give him a home."

Bono sprang on top of a scratching post next to

Lydia. Adopting a classic pose for a few seconds, he reminded me of a sculpture overlooking a European square. I was relieved he could actually sit still. He dipped his head, inviting Lydia to scratch his forehead. I wasn't looking at him so much as the effect he was having on my daughter. As she clucked and cooed over him, he was bringing out a nurturing side I hadn't seen in her before.

Sadie lowered the tuxedo cat to the floor and crouched next to Lydia. The young women raised their hands for a tentative pat. For a moment it looked as if Bono was going to reward their adulation with a lick. But the cat sprang off his haunches and sailed away.

"I come here every day just to visit Bono," Sadie said, looking after him wistfully. "He has a great personality. I'd love to adopt him, but the medical costs are way beyond me."

When I asked if Bono had ever had a home, Jon said the cat was too socialized not to have lived with humans before.

"But he hasn't had one-on-one interaction with people for a long time," he added. "He's going to freak out with you to begin with. Keep him in a small space like a bathroom for the first couple of days. Take it slow. Don't push the relationship. He may hiss."

It seemed our relationship with Bono was going to be complicated. As if that wasn't enough to deal with, Jon added that the cat, who was almost certainly going to be a handful, would need medication twice daily. He scooped Bono off the floor, and held him in the same position Philip used with Jonah. Except Jon's grip was tighter and the paws were tucked firmly down. He made it look a breeze, tilting the cat's head back, prying the jaws open and popping the pill in. If we had any problems with the technique, he said, all we'd have to do is hide a tablet in a slice of fresh chicken and Bono would wolf it down.

"He could gain a pound or two," Jon added, as Bono wriggled out of his grasp and darted away. "He's a fussy eater."

Bono certainly was a scrawny feline. His ribs were clearly visible under his shaved skin. His fur had a dull, lifeless texture of steel wool. Though his eyes were beautiful, they had an oily sheen that didn't look healthy. Being so small and at the bottom of the food chain in the shelter, the cat burned up a lot of nervous energy, Jon said.

"He's never going to leave this place," he continued. "The best you can do for him is to give him a holiday, even if it's just till the weekend."

I asked how much longer Bono was expected to live. When Jon said about three years the boulder in my chest lurched and turned to butter. It was a tough prognosis for such a spirited animal. Any chance of negotiating my way out of fostering him had disappeared faster than a tom cat up a dark alley. Besides, Lydia was captivated.

"You can bring him back in a day or two if it doesn't work out," Jon said.

"Oh really?" I asked, trying to hide my enthusiasm for the idea. "He does seem a bit of a handful."

"No, he's not!" Lydia said, flashing me a disapproving look.

"He's just a bit excited, aren't you boy? We're going to love having him." Jon asked us to leave the room while he wrangled Bono into a carry case. It was a worrying sign. I wondered if a lasso was required.

Back in the reception area, we watched Sadie load Bono's food into a bag. She explained that while he liked the crunchy dry stuff, it was important for him to eat the canned fish because it contained medication that was good for his kidneys. She added a bottle of pills, and handed me a soft, high-walled cat bed shaped like an igloo. I figured it had been carefully chosen for a creature who might want to hide from the world. Jon emerged from the cat room wearing a triumphant grin.

"Call me anytime," he said, presenting Lydia with the cat carrier complete with passenger. "Let him run the relationship. Anything you can give him is more than he's used to. Talk to him. The sound of the human voice works wonders. When we get feral kittens in, we often read to them."

Not for the first time, I was humbled by the

dedication of animal welfare workers. Reading to kittens indeed.

Jon seemed reluctant for us to leave the building with his beloved animal. I wondered if I'd be doing us both a service if I offered to let Bono stay behind. But Lydia was halfway out the door with the cat carrier.

"And remember," Jon called after us. "He's gonna be cranky. Keep him in a confined space for at least twenty-four hours."

As Mrs. Lincoln said to Abraham on the way to the theater, this was going to be a laugh a minute.

*Chapter Nine*

# WITH OR WITHOUT YOU

*Velvet paws are
fragile yet strong.*

We opted to walk the six blocks from Bideawee to our studio apartment. Lydia clucked and fussed as she toted Bono's carrier past the UN Building. Two golden eyes gazed out through the mesh. He was unnervingly quiet. A couple of times I asked her to stop and to check he was still alive. The orbs stared back at us warily. Maybe he was plotting escape. That would be a disaster. Even though Bono didn't have a home, there was no doubt the people at Bideawee cared deeply for him.

After he'd arrived at Bideawee with a kidney infection, the shelter invested a considerable sum in his veterinary care. His five-star treatment had included antibiotics and fluids. I was impressed Bideawee's commitment to this strange-looking cat was so unwavering. But the organization has a long history of going beyond the norm to help animals in need.

Though it takes a stretch of imagination to picture farm animals and horses plodding down Fifth Avenue, they were a common sight back in the early 1900s. To make the animals' working days easier, Bideawee installed and maintained water troughs throughout the city. A 1907 photo of a weary carriage horse drinking deeply from a Bideawee barrel is as heartwarming today as it was over a hundred years ago.

As we escorted Bono into our lives, it was strange to think none of this would be happening if it hadn't been for the remarkable and well-traveled Mrs. Flora D'Auby Jenkins Kibbe. More than 100 years ago, on a trip to France, she was inspired by the work of a radical dog refuge, Barrone d'Herpents. Instead of destroying stray dogs, as was the common practice, the refuge collected them from all over Paris and cared for them until they could be given new homes.

Mrs. Kibbe took the idea back to New York where, by the end of 1903, she was caring for abandoned animals from a modest building near her Manhattan home. She called it Bideawee (meaning "stay a while" in Scottish).

By the time her canine collection exceeded 200, her neighbors started complaining about the barking and she was forced to move her animals to a series of temporary shelters. Just when it was looking as if Mrs. Kibbe's vision might dwindle into history, New Yorkers dug deep and gave Bideawee the permanent home it still has today at 410 East 38th Street.

The organization has since expanded to include two centers on Long Island, along with memorial grounds, where thousands of treasured pets are laid to rest.

Through the wonderful work of Bideawee, Mrs. Kibbe's ghost continues to smile over New York's lost and needy creatures. The most recent beneficiary of her policy of never euthanizing an animal unless it's in the final stages of incurable illness or suffering was inside the carrier at the end of Lydia's arm.

The food and medicine bags were light enough for me to carry, but the cat bed was unwieldy. I was relieved when Lydia put Bono's carrier down on the sidewalk to push strands of hair back from her face.

I assumed the tears glistening on her cheeks were a reaction to the icy wind coming off the East River, and waited for her to shrug them off. But then I realized she was actually weeping. I hadn't seen my self-contained daughter cry in years. Even though she was adult and far better educated than me, I was still programmed to be mother duck, wanting to envelop her in my wings to heal every hurt.

"What's the matter?" I asked, setting the cat bed and bags of pet food down on the sidewalk and bundling her into my arms.

"Three years," she said, sobbing, "It's not fair. He's a beautiful cat. Life's so . . . fragile."

Animals like Bono are the invisible victims of natural disasters all too often. Not so long ago, in my homeland New Zealand, Christchurch was the country's most stately and unruffled city.

Modeled on English tradition, a handsome stone cathedral dominated an attractive square in the city center. With the river Avon meandering past gracious buildings and parkland, Christchurch seemed solid as the stones that shaped the cathedral itself.

All that changed at lunchtime on February 22, 2011. A massive earthquake toppled the cathedral's steeple, decimated buildings, and claimed 185 human lives. Years later, the city is still piecing itself together after the physical and emotional devastation.

The number of animals crushed under the rubble was never counted, and the earthquake's impact on those that survived was enormous. Cats vanished for days on end, dogs fled in panic. Even smaller animals were traumatized. Caged birds batted their wings against their cages and pecked at their feathers.

Some people risked their lives breaking through cordoned off areas to rescue pets from collapsed buildings. Others were too fraught and focused on piecing their own lives together to worry about their four-legged friends.

As the dust settled in the days following the earthquake, hundreds of bewildered cats and dogs were taken off the streets and housed in shelters. Sadly, not all pets were reunited with their owners. Some people, whose lives and houses were in tatters, didn't feel able to take their animals back. Many pets were euthanized.

Like his Christchurch cousins, Bono was a casualty of a catastrophic event of dimensions beyond human control.

He was a mystery cat. No one at Bideawee seemed to know the exact circumstances he'd been rescued from, or how he'd been given that name, but it suited him to the spikes of his jaunty mane.

On October 22, 2012, his human owner would have been unaware of the trough of low air pressure sucking moisture from the Caribbean Sea off the coast of distant Nicaragua.

However, there's a chance that Bono, along with 14 million other felines on the eastern seaboard, sensed a subtle change in the air pressure. The connection between cats and climate has been acknowledged for centuries. The father of smallpox inoculation, Dr. Edward Jenner, paid homage to feline weather forecasters in his poem "Signs of Rain": "Puss on the hearth, with velvet paws Sits wiping o'er her whiskered jaws."

Long before Jenner wrote those lines, sailors kept a weather eye on the ship's cat. To them the seafaring feline was more than just a rat catcher and reminder of cozy fireplaces at home. When they saw the resident feline pawing her face, they knew rough weather was over the horizon. There have been so many reports of cats wiping their faces and ears before a storm, it's thought the electromagnetic changes and low atmospheric pressure bring on a type of migraine. If it's true, the wiping of the face and ears seems logical.

Other nautical superstitions are less feasible. If a cat tried to abandon ship or take her kittens ashore, sailors panicked because it meant trouble lay ahead. A sneezing cat meant rain, a frisky feline was a sign wind was coming, and if a cat licked its fur against the grain, a hailstorm was in the making. Some sailors even believed a feline could create a storm with magic stored in her tail. No doubt generations of cats did nothing to make them believe otherwise.

Though many Europeans shunned black cats as unlucky, British sailors prized them as good omens. With his panache, Bono would have made an excellent ship's mascot.

The Atlantic hurricane season was particularly tumultuous in 2012. Many scientists pointed a finger at global warming. Hurricanes are fueled on warmth, and off the east coast of the United States, the ocean's surface temperature was much higher than usual.

As the storm hurtled toward Jamaica at 80 mph, it was christened Sandy—a benign name reminiscent of beach towels and sunscreen. Two days later, the cyclone raged across Haiti claiming more than fifty human lives in floods and mudslides. It whirled on to Cuba and eventually left the Caribbean with a death toll of seventy to its name.

Witnessing the devastation on their TV screens in the comfort of their living rooms, most New Yorkers would have assumed the storm would conform to the usual pattern, heading out to sea before shrinking to a mere puff over the steely Atlantic. But as Sandy churned north off the coast of Georgia and the Carolinas, meteorologists noticed an unusual combination of atmospheric conditions. The hurricane made a sharp turn and morphed into a super storm raging across 1,000 miles with Baltimore, Washington, Philadelphia, and New York in its path. To make a dangerous situation deadlier, Sandy's arrival was due to coincide with a full moon and exceptionally high tides.

On the eve of the storm, Bono's feline sensors would have gone into overdrive. Instinct would have urged him to run away and hide. On October 29, when Sandy struck Long Island, the roar of the wind and pounding rain was harrowing enough for human ears. For a sensitive cat like Bono it would have been excruciating. His world would have exploded into a surreal nightmare.

Across the water, in Lower Manhattan, fourteen-foot high waves surged over the sea wall at the Battery. The Hugh L. Carey Tunnel (connecting Manhattan to Brooklyn) was flooded, along with parts of the city's subway system.

Four miles farther up the island in Chelsea, Michaela's apartment building was engulfed and left without power or water. Throngs of people fled her neighborhood to stay with friends in less affected parts of the city. But Michaela refused to leave her cats.

At times her apartment must have felt like a deserted island surrounded by undrinkable water. Limited quantities of potable water were available at street level, however. For several days, Michaela and Gene lugged buckets up eighteen flights of stairs to three of the most pampered felines in the city.

Over on Long Island, Bono wasn't so lucky. Watching videos of the storm's impact there, I tried to imagine what he'd been through. If he'd been living in one of the beachside houses, his owners would most likely have evacuated. Perhaps they tried to take him with them but couldn't find the frightened creature. How heartbreaking it must have been if they'd been forced to leave him behind while fleeing for their own safety.

He'd have huddled alone in the darkness, paralyzed with fear as walls shook and windows shattered. A blast of wind may have torn the back door off its hinges. As air was sucked out of the house, a wave two-feet high would have surged up from the waterfront and bashed the front door down. As water gushed through the house, tossing tables and chairs about like toys, Bono would have had to summon every ounce of his animal wit.

Once the storm had passed, I pictured rescue workers wading through an upside-down world where roofs of cars could be seen in the sea and boats lay on their sides in the main street. Perhaps a volunteer noticed a small, bedraggled creature draped over the branch of a tree. The animal was so still, its dark fur flat and matted, she assumed it was dead. But when she reached for the fragile body, its eyes opened and fixed her with an amber gaze.

Maybe, as she slid him into a cat carrier, the radio on the rescue truck was playing "With or Without You." That would solve any debate over what to call the latest storm victim. Whatever his name was before the storm, the cat was dubbed Bono.

It was proving a big year for name changes. The hurricane that claimed at least fifty-three lives and thousands of homes around New York was so devastating, the name Sandy was struck off the list of potential titles for future cyclones.

Thanks to the extraordinary work of animal organizations and Facebook campaigns, hundreds of pets were reunited with their families. Sadly, Bono wasn't one of them.

## Chapter Ten

# HOLY SMOKE

*A cat can be an angel
or a devil—or both.*

Lydia regained composure as we climbed the steps to the red door. Slipping the key into the heart-shaped lock, I was still wondering how a homeless cat could reduce her to tears. In her working life as a trainee psychologist back home, she dealt with harrowing human stories every day.

"Bono doesn't know he has three years to live," I said, as she carried her precious cargo up the first flight of stairs.

Thoughts flashed back to the doctor's surgery. When she told me the cancer growth in my right breast was large, the prospect of dying filled the room with leaden weight. I didn't have the courage to ask those words every human dreads saying—"How long have I got?" But she could see it on my face. She wrote a prescription for sleeping pills to get me through the next few days and said they needed to do more tests. I closed in on myself that day and focused on survival. Though my body had since recovered, I was still in an emotional fox hole.

Animals have the ability to pad lightly and with an open heart into each moment. They do not regard their lives as a line with a beginning, middle, and ending. The creaks and groans of later life are little more than passing inconvenience. However sick Bono was now, he was living the adventure to the fullest and without self-pity, simply until it stopped. I had a lot to learn from him. "Three years is a long time to a cat," I added. "Besides, anything can happen . . ."

I reminded her of our physiotherapist friend, Stephen, and his part kelpie dog Millie. Stephen was devastated when a vet told him Millie had two months to live. The vet had overlooked the fact Stephen has a special affinity for failing bodies, both human and animal. On a diet of organic meat and unadulterated devotion, Millie was still thriving five years later.

"If he finds a good home," I said, puffing up the second flight. "He could live for ages."

*Oh yeah,* the inner cynic piped up. *This city's packed with saints begging to adopt a cat that's going to cost them a Kardashian's ransom in vet's fees, pee all over their apartment and then snuff it.*

My live-in critic introduced himself (it was always a male voice) when I was at journalism school more than forty years earlier. He'd come in handy a few times, especially when I'd been working in the aggressively sexist environment of newsrooms. The witty asides and sneering negativity felt like a protective coating from the more shocking aspects of human behavior.

130

Like most smart-asses though, the inner cynic vanished when times were hard. He offered no consolation through the death of a child, cancer, or the loss of friends, who were starting to fade away with sobering regularity. Though I managed to repress the voice for a while during the spiritual nineties, I never succeeded in getting rid of him completely.

I stopped on a shadowy landing to catch my breath and examine a DO NOT SLAM DOORS! notice scribbled in angry red capitals and duct-taped to a battered-looking door. Whoever lived in there was directly underneath our studio. They must have suffered under the reign of the previous tenants.

After taking a deep breath, I scooped the cat bed and food bags into my arms, plowed up the last flight, and punched the number code in our door lock. Bono peered inquisitively through the wires of his cat carrier as Lydia placed it on the floor. He seemed calm. Lydia and I exchanged looks. We both ached to let him out to explore his temporary home. But Jon's instructions had been clear.

"Guess he'll have to go in the Bunker for a day or two," I said.

"But this place is tiny," Lydia said, waving her arms until her fingertips almost touched the walls on both sides of the room. "And he's so passive. Can't we let him out just for a few minutes?"

True, by Australian standards the studio wasn't much bigger than a birdcage. No doubt Jon gave the same advice to everyone he sent home with a cat. Unlike the wild, bouncing Bono we'd seen at Bideawee, he seemed to have become a different animal. He was placid, almost unnervingly quiet. When I peered into the carrier, a cherub gazed back at me.

What could possibly go wrong? I nodded.

Lydia squeezed the latch on the cat carrier. It sprang open with alarming speed as a ball of black wool burst out, and whirled about the room. Ears flattened against his scalp, eyes ablaze, the cat spun past us in a blur.

Lydia prepared to dive for him as he hurtled toward her, but he made an artful detour at the coffee table and circled back to the center of the room, building up speed like a hurricane.

"Stop!" I yelled, pointlessly at the spiraling force of nature that bore no resemblance to the playful mini lion we'd collected from Bideawee. "You're supposed to be *sick!*"

He spun faster and faster, past the coffee table, sofa, fireplace, coffee table, sofa . . .

I made a grab for him as he galloped, scooting past my knees. It was the first time I'd touched him. The fur on his torso felt coarse and warm, like sheep's wool. His ribs were hard and sharp. He slithered out of my hands.

Having known a few hyperactive children, I've

learned if you keep your cool and refuse to get sucked into their manic state, small creatures run out of energy and calm down—eventually.

*Coffee table, sofa, fireplace, coffee table . . .*

Any moment now, Bono would collapse exhausted in a humble ball of fur.

*Sofa, fireplace, coffee table, sofa . . .*

The cat accelerated, toppling the vase of daffodils and spilling them onto the floor. Then, to our horror and disbelief, he shot up the fireplace.

Lydia and I shared looks of astonishment. We emitted a simultaneous cry as clouds of rubble and dust avalanched down the void into the room. The only evidence of Bono was a black lion's tail, dangling like a doorbell through a curtain of dust from inside the chimney.

The room fell spookily silent. Particles of soot and plaster surfed the watery sunlight. Lydia and I stared at the tail.

"Do you think I should pull it?" I asked.

Lydia didn't answer, but her cheeks were flushed. A cat's tail is a nursery of nerve endings. It contains up to twenty-three bones, which is impressive considering there are only seven in a giraffe's neck. Pulling a tail, even to rescue its owner, almost certainly qualified as animal cruelty. On the other hand, it might save his life.

We heard a shifting sound from inside the chimney. It was followed by another plume of plaster billowing out of the fireplace. My hopes lifted. Maybe Bono had come to his senses and was trying to turn around and come back down.

To my dismay, the tail became shorter. We stood helpless as the cat clawed farther up the cavity until all we could see was the scruffy ball at the end of his tail.

It was incredible he'd managed to squeeze into such a narrow, vertical tunnel. But, to the regret of millions of mice, cats have famously "floating shoulders" that enable them to shimmy into any space wide enough to fit their whiskers.

Silence. It seemed Bono had encountered a blockage in the chimney and couldn't move farther up, or for that matter, down. He was stuck. I could almost hear his brain whirring up there. Lydia was on the brink of tears again.

"He'll be all right," I assured her. "He's a street cat."

One good thing about a feline with an enigmatic past is you can invent any kind of history for him.

Crouched at the entrance to the chimney, I bristled with panic. These antics could bring down the entire building. If not, Bono was likely to endure a horrible end up there, squeezed between bricks and starving to death. We'd lie in bed at night listening to his pitiful meows . . . until they stopped.

There was a scrabbling sound. A fresh cascade of debris landed on my boots. I stepped back. The stones were getting larger. As a piece of broken brick crashed on the floor, the end of Bono's tail moved sideways and then disappeared.

A nanosecond later in a hailstorm of rubble, a small animal tumbled down into the room. White with dust, eyes bulging and teeth bared, it resembled a mythical creature from an Indonesian carving. As it torpedoed though my legs, I grabbed it. Holding it in a wrestling grip, I carried it to the Bunker and shut it in.

Lydia swept the rubble and stuffed the chimney with plastic bags, while I opened a can of cat food. We had no chance of dispensing that crazed animal's medication in the way Jon had demonstrated. I concealed a white tablet in the mush and tiptoed to the Bunker door. Not a sound came from inside. In a single movement, I wedged the door open, shoved the bowl into the darkness, and shut it.

All three of us needed a time out.

*Chapter Eleven*

# Shopping with Mother

*Inside every pussycat
a tiger lurks.*

Jon's warning that Bono's "transition phase" could be challenging was the understatement of the year. The cat had nearly demolished our building. As we stepped outside onto the street, my hands were still shaking. I quietly counted the hours until the weekend, the soonest Jon had suggested Bono's "holiday" with us could end. I'd be needing a health retreat by then.

After months of wintry sleep, the city was shaking itself awake to spring. We stopped to admire boxes of tulips, their pink and yellow lips pouting at the sky.

Women unbuttoned their coats to flaunt brightly colored blouses. Even the handbag sellers on our corner were smiling. Though we'd barely had time to explore our neighborhood, we soon realized it was a microcosm of everything we needed.

"Oh look!" I cried. "A stationery shop."

On the corner across from the handbag sellers, I could make out a window display of greeting cards for every imaginable life event.

"People email these days," Lydia said, trailing after me as I bustled into the store.

"I know, but I still think there's nothing like

a carefully chosen card with a handwritten message."

Oh dear. I was lecturing. We paused in the Sympathy section to examine an impressive range of cards for people who had lost pets. Not so long ago, a cat was just a cat. When it died, you were expected to get over it in 20 minutes. Now even Hallmark was acknowledging the importance of pets in people's lives.

Toward the back of the store, an entire corner was dedicated to *Frozen*. Lydia rolled her eyes while I dived into a mountain of Elsa and Ana trinkets.

"The girls will love these!" I said, gathering up bunches of key rings and pencils.

"Are you sure the *Frozen* characters are good role models?" she asked.

I had no idea. All I could think of was Annie and Stella back home belting out "Let It Go!" until people begged for mercy.

Sated on *Frozen*, we plunged into the sea of traffic on 44th Street. We were both hungry so we entered a vast deli that doubled as an all-day café. After loading salads on our plates, we were taken aback when the tired-looking checkout operator with a Hispanic accent insisted we weigh them. Nobody weighs their food in Australia, at least not until it's sitting in rolls on their hips.

A cop with a paunch equivalent to an eight-month pregnancy hunched over his coffee cup and gazed at the street as if nothing would surprise him. At the next table, a couple sat opposite each other and shouted into their phones. I liked the everyday grittiness of the deli and the people who went there.

Afterward, we walked past the fruit shop next door. The Indian man who'd served us the night before waved from behind a bank of flowers. Far from being scary, violent New York, this place was positively friendly.

"Let's say hello to Doris," Lydia said as we approached the pet supply shop.

Bluebell was dozing in the window, her tail curved neatly around her front feet.

"Not yet," I said.

Doris would be shocked to hear of Bono's disappearing up the chimney act. She'd label us the world's most incompetent cat lovers.

We strode past the hardware shop. I couldn't face the girls in there, either. I steered Lydia around a corner down a gentle slope past cafés and diners toward Grand Central Station.

I began to realize the reason so many New Yorkers look as if they have stepped out of hair salons is they probably have. There were more pocket-sized beauty salons, nail bars, and dry cleaners than I could count. Across the street, a supermarket overshadowed a computer gadget store, where I hoped to someday find a 12-year-old who would help end my Wi-Fi drought.

Even more alluring was an authentic-looking clinic offering acupuncture and Chinese medicine. With any luck, a few artfully placed needles and a massage would down-age my knee.

"Oooh, look!" Lydia said, stopping outside a bakery window packed with sumptuous pastries.

"Those raspberry tarts are to die for!" I said.

But she'd hardly noticed them.

"They've got free Wi-Fi!" she said, pointing at a discreet sign.

"Don't you want a raspberry tart?" I asked.

"Okay, I guess we'll have to buy something to get the Wi-Fi," she said. Before we knew it, we were inside sitting at a scrubbed wooden table and feverishly checking our emails. I itched to call Philip. He wouldn't believe a fraction of the things we'd been through in the past forty-eight hours. But there was no point. He'd be fast asleep with Jonah curved like a croissant next to his knees.

The only downside of my raspberry tart was the sign over the counter advertising the fact it contained 510 calories. Back home, cakes hardly ever confess how fat they're going to make you. The tart landed in front of me with a guilt-inducing clunk.

"Delicious!" I said, digging into it with a fork. "Want to go halves?"

Like most naturally slim people, Lydia could take or leave a pastry.

"Please," I said. "You'd be doing me a favor."

"Oh all right," she said, graciously raising a spoon.

The cappuccino was good, but I was hankering after a full octane Australasian latte served by a barista in a man bun.

I planned to take Lydia inside Grand Central Station to show her the immense cathedral-like hall with its eggshell-colored ceiling, displaying the constellations in elegant gold leaf, but she disappeared into a women's boutique near the entrance. I was more than pleased to hang around while she reveled in trying on skirts, tops, and shoes. She'd missed out on years of shopping.

"What do you think?" she asked, emerging from a changing booth wearing a creamy blouse with a flouncy collar.

I caught my breath when I saw the neckline plunging between her breasts. It was the last thing I'd have expected her to choose.

"Looks great!" I said. "What will you wear with it?"

"Oh, these pants will do," she said gazing down at her jeans.

I rifled through a pile of skirts and held one up. "How about this?"

Lydia twisted her mouth. It was knee length and probably too short for her taste, but I saw no harm in expanding her horizons.

"I was thinking more this," she said, reaching for a brown handkerchief posing as a skirt.

I waited outside the booth, anxious she might have an identity crisis in there. When she pulled the curtain aside, a beautiful, faun-like creature stepped toward me. The cream blouse glowed against her skin, and the miniskirt made the most of her legs.

"You look beautiful!" I said. "Now all you need are the shoes."

Lydia demurred, saying she'd spent enough already.

"My treat," I said, pointing her at the stairs leading to the shoe section.

For someone who'd spent years in and out of a monastery, my daughter had a highly developed sense of style. She chose elegant, tan ankle boots with a discreet gold chain around each of the heels.

She thanked me several times over as we left the store on a rare and wonderful thing for her—a retail high.

"You know my friend Maggie," Lydia said, as we joined the sidewalk throng.

Keeping up with my offspring's friends is always a challenge.

"She has a pedometer," Lydia went on. "Maggie found out she takes more steps when she's shopping with her mum than when she exercises on purpose."

"Really?" I said. "Well, we'd better keep going." I was grateful for any excuse to delay finding out what Bono was up to.

We headed on to Macy's, Herald Square, where I was expecting her to be overwhelmed by the scale of one of the world's largest department stores.

A religion more than a store, Macy's has a calendar of festivals, the most famous being the Thanksgiving Day Parade, which has been featured in countless movies and TV shows, from *Sweet Charity* to *Friends*. More than eight thousand participants march, float, and pulsate their way through Manhattan's streets. Christmastime is no less exciting, with dazzling window displays and thousands of shoppers taking the elevator to Santaland on the eighth floor.

A spring flower show featuring a life-sized elephant statue bedecked with blossoms was in full swing while we were there, but we never found it.

The moment we stepped through Macy's doors into a heated labyrinth of leather goods I wanted to turn and run for fresh air. But Lydia became calm and clear-eyed, like a predator prowling a fertile plain. She stepped softly through rows of brightly colored purses of every conceivable shape and size. I trailed after her until she stopped at a display of animal print bags, which my penny-wise daughter pointed out, were reduced by 30 percent.

If I'd gone out to buy her a handbag, I'd have

opted for something in line with her classic taste—modest and beige. But New York was having a radical impact on my daughter. She was entranced by a shoulder bag in a giraffe-skin pattern with tan trimmings. As she took it from its hook and opened the zipper to reveal a scarlet lining, her face lit up. Conservative Lydia of the neutral ballet pumps and thrift shop cardigans was becoming a fashion tigress. We bought it.

"What do you think Bono's doing?" she asked.

I was trying not to think about him.

"He'll be having a rest," I said.

We rode a befuddling number of escalators. By the time we reached the children's clothing department, my feet were aching and my head was spinning like a potato in a microwave. Still, I found enough stamina to pick up a couple of dresses for the granddaughters.

"Would you mind taking these back with you?" I asked Lydia.

"Don't you want to take them back yourself to give them to the girls?"

I didn't like to tell her that at this rate my granddaughters could be teenagers by the time I gave up on New York and went home.

With a pang of guilt, I went on to the men's department. Philip always liked a new shirt. I sifted through a pile and picked out a jaunty red checked one, a good weight for the Australian winter ahead. If I stayed on in New York, it might not be possible to deliver it in person. Still, it would be easy enough to wrap it up and send it to him from the post office next to Grand Central.

"What about Ramon?" I called to Lydia, who was drifting away.

She looked blank. Maybe they weren't a serious couple, after all.

"Aren't you taking something home for him?" I said fingering a pale purple T-shirt. "What size is he?"

Lydia didn't know.

"Is he anything like my size?" a deep mahogany voice asked.

A breathtakingly handsome African American man smiled at me from the other side of the T-shirt pile. He was draping an identical purple T-shirt across his athletic torso.

"What size are you?" I asked smoothing the cotton against his solid pecs.

"Extra large," he said with a gentle smile. "But sometimes I'm just large."

It had been a long time since I'd thought about sex. Strange how not thinking about it can become almost as habitual as thinking about it. Most of the time I love not thinking about sex. It's empowering. It wasn't until I reached an age when I could be confident 99.99 percent of the population would not dream of regarding me as a sensual being that I was released to drift unmolested through any situation.

147

To all good-looking women who fear the day heads no longer swivel when they enter a room, I say come on in. The water's fabulous. I cannot tell you how refreshing it is to know that any man who approaches me now is, in all sincerity, asking for directions. Or offering to help choose the right sized T-shirt. Not since I was 5 years old and thought mummies and daddies ordered babies from hospitals have I felt so unconstrained.

I can honestly say that since the world became a giant selfie, there's no better place to be than on the sidelines. Not thinking about sex or who I have to impress has freed me up to have a life. My brain is primed for friendship, crosswords, speaking my mind, and talking to birds (if they feel like listening).

That said, I was disturbed at the physical effect this thoughtful young man was having on me. My cheeks were burning. I called Lydia over. We decided Ramon was probably large, thanked the man and bought the T-shirt.

"A bit young for you, isn't he?" Lydia said as we made our way to the sales desk.

"Don't be silly. He thinks I'm his mother."

I hadn't felt so wickedly free since 1969. But then I saw him in the men's shoe section. Philip was standing in front of a mirror inspecting a brand new pair of cowboy boots. Wild West gear was hardly his usual taste. Maybe he was having an identity crisis, too. Not that I was having a crisis. If I was going through anything, it was more of a post-cancer, two-thirds life reinvention.

In a rush of affection, I hurried toward him and was on the point of wrapping my arms around him, cowboy boots and all. Until I realized he didn't look the least bit like the man I loved.

We left Macy's and crossed the street to Victoria's Secret. Not so long ago, Lydia had turned me on to the ultra-comfortable bras she'd been buying from infomercials. Made of beige polyester with straps thick enough to hoist a shipping container, they were comfortable, but hardly alluring. They suited me fine, particularly as underwires aren't recommended for women who have had breast cancer. But I was concerned my Gen Y daughter saw the point of them, too.

The only thing more difficult than imagining that your parents are having sex is to conjure up visions of your children doing it. Still, I didn't want Lydia to miss out on the ecstatic highs—and she had a better chance of achieving them wearing something other than a bra designed for decrepit piano teachers.

A friendly shop assistant directed her to some leopard skin bras trimmed with neon pink lace (it was the year of animal prints). Lydia was quick to try them on and they looked so good, we bought two with matching panties. The turquoise bra I bought for myself wasn't quite so alluring, but it was less utilitarian than the skin-colored boob hammocks at home. I wondered if Philip would notice the difference.

While my daughter's attention was diverted to a flouncy nightie Mum would have called "slutty," I fingered a satin scarlet bra. It was the same size and style as the turquoise one. The likelihood of wearing it in real life was slim, but the encounter in Macy's menswear had unsettled me. Novels have been written about wives on the run, drunk with freedom. They always end up throwing themselves under trains or overdosing on laudanum. Still, this was twenty-first century New York. If I wanted to become a sexagenarian sex kitten, it was my choice. After a quick check that nobody was looking, I tucked the red bra in my shopping basket under the turquoise one.

As the afternoon melted away, we ran out of hands to carry any more bags. I started feeling guilty about the rubbish island that's bigger than Texas floating out in the Pacific. Even if we recycled the bags, they'd probably end up choking fish somewhere.

Lydia was running out of energy, too.

"I'm worried about Bono," she said. Using the Chrysler Building as a point of reference, we made our way back to Second Avenue. Heavy with trepidation, I opened the heart lock to climb the paint-speckled stairs.

## Chapter Twelve

# CAT BALLET

*Happiness
is a sock.*

The studio was eerily silent. Lydia called through the Bunker door, but there was no reply. I wondered if a cat burglar had snuck in and abducted Bono while we were out.

"Do you think he's asleep?" I asked.

"Why don't you take a look?"

As I reached for the handle, the Bunker door exploded open.

"Oh no!" Lydia cried as a black dart sped across the room and disappeared under my bed.

"Come out!" I said, crouching to peer under the bed.

A pair of golden eyes glowered from the shadows and refused to budge.

Lydia lowered herself on to her stomach and wriggled across the floor toward him.

"Hello, Bono boy," she crooned. "Don't be scared. We're going to look after you."

Her tone made me think of a cop talking a suicide case off a bridge.

"Everything's going to be okay," she said.

Lydia's patience with our fugitive was endless.

Superfluous to the interaction, I went to take a look inside the Bunker. I was relieved to see there was a dark stain in the litter box. Though the smell was slightly sour, it was a sign his kidneys were functioning. When I saw the food bowl was empty, I felt a surge of happiness. Our captive had felt comfortable enough to eat. But when I saw the small white pill sitting in the bottom of the bowl, I let out an involuntary groan.

"What's the matter?" Lydia called. I scraped the tablet up and took it to show her.

"He hasn't even licked the thing," I said.

"That's no good," Lydia said, standing up and brushing her trousers off.

"If we don't get a pill into him soon, he'll get sick," I said, tossing the rejected tablet in the bin.

"He's still settling in," Lydia said.

"We'll have to take him back to Bideawee. Jon will think we're a joke."

"Give him time." Lydia was using her psychology skills again.

"Michaela and Vida will think I'm an idiot! Why can't he come out from under there so I can give him his pill?"

"Don't worry," Lydia said. "Let's have dinner. I'll get us some takeout food from that Chinese restaurant."

Alone in the room, I had a feeling I was being watched. Maybe this is all he needs, I thought. If we go about our everyday activities, he'll get used to the sound of our voices, our routines, and maybe become more interested in getting to know us. For now, though, it was clear he wanted us to ignore him. We had no choice but to oblige.

I fiddled with the Skype connection on my laptop. The prepaid USB stick from the computer shop seemed to be working.

"Hello, stranger!" I said.

It was so good to see Philip's face again.

He was in bed waking up to early morning Melbourne. Jonah yowled from the pillow beside him. Somewhere in the background, a tram was rattling down High Street a few yards from our house.

"Still wearing the pajamas," I said.

"I need them. And this," he said, holding up a mohair blanket. "It's freezing here without you. What have you been up to?"

"We found out Michaela's an ice skating goddess and you wouldn't believe what a mess this place was. Honestly, they must've been druggies . . ." Jonah's ears swiveled at the sound of my voice, while my husband listened the way an adult does to a breathless child.

"Oh and then we went to a Holi festival. See? I've still got paint on my arms."

"How's the apartment now?" he asked.

I spun my laptop around the room and gave him a running commentary about the layout and the *West Side Story* fire escape.

"Where's the cat?" he asked, when I paused to take a breath.

I lowered the computer to the floor beside my bed.

"Under there," I said. "He's got beautiful eyes. Can you see him?"

Philip leaned into his computer screen.

"It's too dark," he said.

There was something surreal about my husband being on screen in such familiar surroundings while I felt like Alice in Wonderland on speed. I could almost smell the motionless air of our bedroom back home. It was ages since I'd vacuumed behind that bed. The wall behind him hadn't changed color in at least a decade. In all honesty, the place looked stale.

"Well, I'd better jump in the shower and get off to work," he said, lifting Jonah gently on to the floor.

There'd be a hollow echo through the house as he closed the front door. If I was still at home, Jonah and I would be left to muddle through twelve hours of housework mingled with writing attempts. I was in no hurry to get back. Not if I could spend the rest of my days sipping champagne on the balcony of a little apartment in Soho. We blew hygienic kisses and said good-bye as Lydia arrived with dinner.

As we sat side by side on the sofa forking steamed cabbage from polystyrene containers, we tried to talk about other things, but our thoughts were focused on the reluctant houseguest under my bed.

"We've got to get him back in the Bunker," I said. "Otherwise, he'll never adjust to living here."

"Ssshhh," Lydia said. "He's listening."

It's hard to know how much human language cats understand, but she was right. There were scuffling noises from under the bed as we quietly devised a plan.

With no time to delay, we took our positions. I crouched on one side of the bed while Lydia slithered, commando-like, toward Bono from the other. The cat was too fast for us, however. He bolted out into the room. Lydia took chase. She nearly caught him, but he slid out of her hands with impressive expertise and skidded straight back under the bed. Chasing Bono in and out of hiding places was an endurance sport. Before long, Lydia collapsed on the sofa, while I fell on the bed, hoping the pressure on the mattress wouldn't squash the tenant underneath.

"This is no fun!" I gasped. "Why can't he be friendly?"

Staring up at the purple curtains, I wondered how soon we could take up Jon's offer to return Bono to Bideawee. The cat was clearly miserable living with us.

Even Lydia didn't seem so besotted anymore. She quietly made up her sofa with sheets and the blanket. I asked if she'd like to share the bed with me, but she said she was fine. To tell the truth, I wasn't heartbroken because my bed was so narrow it barely classified as a double.

I took the copy of *Time Out* off the bedside table that doubled as a chest of drawers and salivated over the shows and plays going on just a few blocks away.

"Hey Liddy," I said. "Something called *Kinky Boots* is getting great reviews on Broadway. Shall I see if we can get tickets?"

She was either asleep, or pretending to be. My daughter's lack of interest in musicals was unfathomable.

Next morning we woke to see a small black shape dancing across the floor, at war with one of Lydia's socks. Shaking it by the toe and tossing it in the air, Bono was so deeply engaged in battle, he didn't notice our interest. The previous day's trauma had melted away for him, and now he was delighting in the simple act of fighting a sock. Bono was unwanted and terminally ill, yet he was relishing the fact he was alive right now with a sock for a playmate. I wished I could be such a master at embracing the moment. It would take decades of therapy and spiritual practice for me to reach that level. If only I could be more like Bono and stop fretting over things beyond my control.

He paused and stretched his right back leg out in a perfect arabesque. I'd never seen a cat perform such a balletic move before.

"Oh, he's so *cute!*" Lydia cried.

He froze at the sound of her voice.

"It's all right," she said softly.

Bono dropped the sock and flitted like a shadow into a crevice between the sofa bed's backrest and the wall.

"That's the last we'll see of him today," I said.

Lydia placed her hand at the entrance to Bono's new hiding place and continued talking gently to him. To my astonishment, a dark head emerged and tentatively nudged her fingers with his nose.

It was a touching scene, but if Bono was to survive he needed that pill. Feeling like an evil jailor, I snatched him, carried him to the Bunker, and shut the door behind us. Crouched on the floor, I held him tightly and forced a pill down his gullet. In that horrible moment, I could sense his (understandable) dislike of me. Worse, I felt any chance of him trusting me had gone for good.

## Chapter Thirteen

# THE UNIVERSE IN AMBER

*There's no finer work
of art than a cat.*

The math wasn't difficult. Jon had given us permission to return Bono to Bideawee on the weekend. Today was Wednesday. That left only three more nights of living with a four-legged hermit. There was no shame in it. We would have fulfilled our mission of giving a sick cat a "holiday."

Meantime, I decided to grant Bono's wish of wanting to be ignored, to make the most of the week Lydia had left in New York.

"What say we go to an art museum?" I asked.

My daughter's eyes narrowed. As a little girl, she'd been more interested in climbing doorframes than visiting art galleries. During the religious phase of her late teens and early twenties, she had frowned on artistic expression of any kind.

"What sort of museum?" she said in a tone that implied tooth extraction was involved.

"I think you'll like MoMA," I said. "It's modern and not too big."

Every outstanding gallery seems to start with a group of rich, public-spirited visionaries. In the early 1920s, names like Rockefeller, Goodyear, and Sachs got together with the idea of creating the greatest museum of modern art in the world. Public enthusiasm billowed and the collection rapidly expanded. The gallery had to move to larger quarters three times until it settled in its current Midtown spot in 1939.

Lydia appeared offhand as we lined up in the cold with hundreds of other tourists waiting for the doors to open. Admiring the new giraffe print bag draped over her shoulder, I kept my mouth shut. If this didn't work out, we could always go back to retail therapy.

I've witnessed countless moments of transformation in Lydia—from the round-faced baby taking her first uncertain steps, to the young woman sweeping on stage to accept her university degree. Something equally momentous seemed to happen that day on MoMA's fifth floor when we encountered the three large paintings of Monet's water lilies.

Mesmerized, she lapsed into silence and allowed herself to sink into the master's pools of pastel-colored beauty. Though she didn't say anything, I believe it was the first time she understood the spiritual quality of art. Watching how deeply the paintings moved her, I felt on the edge of tears. If we'd packed up and left New York that afternoon, the journey would have been worth it.

I could understand why Monet devoted the last thirty years of his life to painting the water lilies. Nature becomes more miraculous as you get older and prepare to surrender your body to it. He saw the universe in his magical pond, and painted it nearly 250 times.

Admiring prints of Monet's water lilies on a calendar or table napkin is one thing, but to stand in front of three, each more than six feet long, is to be transported to another world.

As we descended to the lower floors through displays of perplexing twenty-first century creations, Lydia asked me what happened to art. I didn't feel qualified to answer. After a brief stop at the gift shop to pick up postcards of our favorite paintings, we hailed a cab.

"Let's go to the Frick," I said, pressing my luck.

"What's that?"

"It's a smaller museum, with a wonderful collection of old masterpieces."

"How old?" she asked, suspicious.

"You'll find out when we get there," I said. "We can leave if you don't like it."

Skyscrapers perforated clear spring air as the taxi glided through rows of blooming trees on Park Avenue. With New York at her magical best and my daughter opening herself to art, I was on a high.

"I oughta kill you!" a Hummer driver shouted through his open window at our driver, who apparently hadn't moved over to let him into his lane.

We cowered, half expecting Hummer man to raise a revolver, leaving us to mop the cabbie's brain off the sidewalk.

"Bastard," our driver muttered as he pressed the accelerator and swerved ahead at teeth-shattering speed. Once a safe distance from his aggressor, the driver slowed down to explain he was a practicing Buddhist and a pacifist. But he'd lived in the city twenty-seven years so was entitled to use the local lingo.

Lydia quickly overcame her reservations about "old stuff". The wry twist of a mouth in a Gainsborough portrait, or a witty twinkle in the eye of a woman wearing an eighteenth-century wig are reminders people haven't changed. Power, sex, fame, and death are ongoing obsessions.

I was drawn to the works featuring animals. Cats, dogs, and horses are portrayed with great tenderness in paintings three hundred years old. It was comforting to see the connection between humans and their quadruped friends is eternal. The trouble was from every exquisitely painted animal eye, I saw Bono staring back at me. As Monet had admired the universe in his pond, I considered the possibility of comprehending all creation in Bono's amber gaze. Our prisoner was getting to me.

We arrived home to the sound of paws scuffling over floorboards.

"Oh well," I said, watching a pom-pom tail disappear under the bed. "Only two days to go."

Whatever Bono got up to while we were out exploring the city was a mystery. I was disheartened. It was like living with a ghost.

"Till what?" Lydia asked. She was opening a can of cat food.

We'd given up trying to keep Bono in the Bunker. It was pointless. Whenever I opened the door a crack to shove a food bowl in there, he bolted out and refused to be caught.

"Jon said we can take him back to the shelter at the weekend. Remember?"

Lydia looked shocked.

"We can't do that!" she said.

"Let's face it. He's a disaster."

"No, he's not! He's beautiful."

"He just hides under the bed and glowers at us like we're a pair of murderers."

Lydia's eyes became as moist as Monet's pools.

"You say you're a cat person," she said.

"I am, but . . ."

"He needs us." Her voice was ragged with emotion.

"I know, but he's hardly thriving."

"Nobody said it was going to be easy," she said. "Can't we keep him at least until I go home? It's only seven more days."

I could hardly say no. A week would go fast enough.

167

# • • •

Lydia's passion for Bono intensified by the day. As she lay on the floor beside the bed talking to our shadowy guest with endless patience, a tangible bond developed between them.

Bono had a wily street-cat side. Whatever he'd been through, he'd proved himself a survivor. At times he was so silent and still, we forgot he was in the room. As he listened in on our conversations, it seemed the shadow under my bed was finding out everything about us. I wondered what was going on inside his head.

Though he refused to approach Lydia during daylight hours, at night he crept out to sleep on the back of her sofa bed above her head. The moment she woke, he flitted away again.

It was all very touching, but I had more urgent worries.

When I replaced the meal with food that wasn't laced, he treated it with the same disdain. With the cat putting himself on a starvation diet, there was no hope of sneaking medication into his meal. To make things worse, since our ghastly struggle to get the pill down his throat, I was his least favorite human.

There was only one person to call.

"Hi there! How's Bono settling in?" Jon's voice radiated warmth.

It was one of those questions with a long or

short answer. I wasn't about to own up to the chimney incident.

"He's okay. He's drinking lots, but he's stopped eating the canned food you gave us."

"I see." Jon didn't sound at all alarmed.

"The first time was understandable because I'd crushed a pill and spooned it through the mash," I said. "He must have hated the taste of it."

"Have you been able to give him pills manually, the way I showed you?" Jon asked.

"Only once," I said, tears rising in my throat. "He hates me now."

I'd seen cat whisperers at work on TV shows. The problems people have with their cats are almost always due to human failing. I used to look down my nose at the couple whose cat attacked their ankles. Couldn't they see the feline was bored? Now I was as much a wreck as any hapless TV cat owner. I could sense Jon listening carefully, like a psychiatrist, at the end of the line.

"Of course he doesn't hate you," Jon said. There was kindness in every syllable.

"And I can't catch him to have another go. He's too fast on his feet."

Jon had clearly dealt with far more serious problems between cats and people than this. He was so relaxed I wanted to scream.

"I'm a foster mother failure," I added, half hoping he'd insist we return Bono immediately.

Instead, he laughed in a comforting way. "No, you're not," he said. "Just sneak a pill inside a piece of fresh chicken breast, or turkey. He'll love that."

"Are you sure?"

"You're doing great," he said. "And call me anytime. If I'm not here you can always talk to another staff member."

The cat whisperer's confidence was so reassuring, I thought I might have a chance of living up to it—if only he'd offer to move in with us for a week.

## Chapter Fourteen

# LOVE IN HIDING

*A cat rewards affection
only when he is ready.*

Loving someone is easy. Getting them to love you back can be complicated. People have fought, died, and created the greatest art for it. From what I know, the more desperately you ache for another's affection, the faster they will run.

I still cannot fathom how Philip and I fell for each other. It was one of those rare, explosive events, like an asteroid crashing into Earth. Being eight years older with two kids in tow, I was hardly a catch. And he was fresh out of the army with a body straight out of a Greek sculpture gallery. With us being opposites in so many ways, there were countless times it would have been logical for us to take off in separate directions. I'd be lying if I said there haven't been a few occasions when it looked as if that might happen.

How we'd managed to stick together for more than two decades was even more mysterious than the falling in love part. Except now I'd claimed time-out, and we were on opposite sides of the world. He was up to god knows what in Melbourne while I whiled away my freedom pining for the affections of a sick cat.

Being a woman, I've listened to countless true stories of rejected passion. Love has become another consumer item. People think if they want it badly enough, and are willing to pay a high enough price, they'll get it. They try too hard, expose too much of themselves too soon. Quite often, all they're left with is a shredded ego and a pile of psychologists' bills.

The trick, I think, is to observe the skills of seducers and animal whisperers. If you sincerely want someone to fall for you, first signal your admiration, then create a benign space around yourself and step back a little. This allows the other person—or creature—to observe you and decide if they are interested. It gives them room to move forward. That way they will think *they* have chosen *you*. If they are repelled by your initial show of appreciation, well then you have not humiliated yourself entirely.

After Jon's pep talk, I decided to stop beating myself up over Bono. We'd had a bad start, but we could move on from that. When the cat cringed at the sound of my booming voice, I wouldn't take it personally anymore or try to imitate Lydia's soft sing-song tone. He'd have to get used to the fact that, for all my faults, this was me.

I wasn't asking much of him in return, apart from acceptance—and a willingness to swallow the occasional pill. We both had wounds, insecurities, and question marks over the future. From now on, I would chill out so the cat and I could find a way to get along together, with Lydia as our ambassador, at least for a few more days.

Besides, we couldn't send him back to the shelter until Michaela had set eyes on him.

"Do you think the place still stinks?" I asked, straightening our gallery postcards on the mantelpiece.

"I can't tell," Lydia said, snapping her bed back into the shape of a sofa. "Should we get some air freshener?"

"Flowers would be better."

I hurried across the street and brought back arms full of heavily scented lilacs. We placed them in strategic positions—outside the Bunker, next to the bed, and (to discourage a repeat performance from Bono) in front of the fireplace.

"What happens now?" Lydia asked.

"We wait, I suppose."

"I mean how does Michaela get up the stairs without a key? Isn't there some kind of doorbell?"

We'd never had a visitor before.

"I haven't seen one. I'll go downstairs and wait for her on the street."

An explosive buzz shook the room.

"The doorbell!" Lydia said. "There has to be a way of opening the downstairs door from here."

I watched her stab buttons on a disused looking

keypad beside our doorway and wondered what made her think that would work. She must have seen too many episodes of *Friends*. I stumbled down the stairs to greet our guest.

"Not the greatest apartment in the world," I said, escorting Michaela into our studio. "But big enough to swing a cat."

Michaela seemed momentarily taken back by the modesty of our surroundings.

"Oh," she said, regaining composure. "It's . . . lovely."

The coffee we made was passable. The organic fig biscuits were crisp. But there was an amber-eyed elephant in the room.

"Where's Bono?" Michaela asked, batting her eyelashes in anticipation.

I tried to summon a socially acceptable answer, or maybe even a white lie.

"Under the bed."

"Oh."

"He's shy, but he comes out when we're away," I said, trying to sound casual. "At least, we think he does."

"He's magical," Lydia chimed in. "Come see."

My daughter dropped to her knees beside the bed, lay on her stomach, and beckoned Michaela over. Watching the elegantly suited editor lie down and adopt the same position beside her, I wished I'd thought to mop the floor.

"Oh, he *is* adorable!" Michaela said.

As she stood up and dusted herself off, Michaela didn't seem at all disappointed. She agreed with Lydia that he was indeed a beautiful cat.

"I've got some wonderful news," Michaela said. "Vida has been working very hard and she's scored you a portal on the *Huffington Post*. It's really quite a coup."

Of course I'd heard of the *Huffington Post*, the online newspaper set up by Ariana Huffington in 2005. Millions of eyeballs scrolled its pages every day. But a portal sounded like something out of *Star Trek*. I had enough trouble posting on Facebook, let alone diving into a portal.

"We think it would be great if you wrote a blog for them about Bono," Michaela said, beaming megawatts of optimism.

"If we can stir up some interest, maybe we can find him a permanent home."

At that moment, the usual tightness in my shoulders upgraded to an ache.

"You mean, someone who'll adopt him?" I asked.

Not only were we to foster this terminally ill cat, I was supposed to write a *Huffington Post* blog that would find him an actual home? What did Michaela and Vida imagine I could say about a cat who refused to come out from under the bed?

"I'm not much of a blogger," I said. "In fact, I have no idea how to go about it."

"Vida's a tech wizard," Michaela said. "Her team of marketing mavens will help you log on. Or you can just email the pieces to her and she'll put them up for you."

I grabbed another fig biscuit off the plate, chomped it in two bites and waited for the calming effects of a sugar high to kick in. There were approximately three people in the world who'd read anything I wrote for the *Huffington Post*. Two of them would have cats already. To hope anyone might fall in love with our antisocial housemate enough to offer him a home was beyond whimsical.

"Don't worry," Michaela said. "I've got a good feeling about this."

I wondered if General Custer said the same thing when he heard Chief Sitting Bull was waiting for him.

# Chapter Fifteen

# IN PRAISE OF MELANCHOLY

*Sometimes a cat craves*
*nothing more than solitude.*

One of the reasons Lydia had wanted to visit New York was to walk the same streets as her literary hero, Nora Ephron. Sadly, the witty, self-effacing author of *Heartburn* (along with magnificent works of journalism) had died the previous year. In one of her pieces, Nora made a reference to eyebrow threading as a "fantastic and thrilling" form of hair removal. The practice had yet to arrive in Melbourne in any noticeable way. My daughter had been quick to point out a salon a few doors up from our neighborhood deli. I knew she was keen to undergo the process in homage to Nora, and I was curious. Besides, I wasn't about to discourage her from exploring vanity as a concept.

Peering through the salon window, we watched a therapist insert a string of white cotton between her teeth. She then bent over her client and manipulated the string into a sort of cat's cradle. Client and therapist were deep in concentration.

This ancient practice, which began in Asia thousands of years ago, looked enjoyable compared to the agonies of waxing. I have often wondered what kind of sadist dreamed up the idea of smothering hot wax above someone's eyelids before ripping it off, along with multiple layers of skin.

We bounced into the salon to emerge thirty minutes later chastened, our faces red and stinging. Compared to eyebrow threading, waxing's a holiday in Fiji. Still, I had to admire Lydia's brows, which now formed perfect, elegantly shaped arches.

We both wanted to look our best for our big night on the town. Michaela had invited us out, along with Gene, to contra dancing, which she assured us was a simple form of folk dance imported from the British Isles. While musicians played reels and jigs, the caller instructed the dancers in a series of moves that sent them spinning around the room in intricate, aerobic patterns. I noticed that the dancers smiled and laughed a lot, and a good deal of flirting was taking place.

The event was held in the basement of a church hall in Chelsea. At first glance, it seemed a perfectly normal get-together by New York standards—until I noticed the athletic woman wearing an ankle-length blue velvet gown and diamante earrings was in fact a handsomely bearded man. Contra dancing was a vigorous and complicated workout. I was hopeless at it and was soon panting on the sidelines. Lydia was awash with suitors asking her onto the floor. She accepted all invitations, and I was delighted to see how much she was enjoying herself.

Content to drink in the spectacle on my own, I hardly noticed an approaching male. He was unusually short with charcoal hair scraped into parallel lines.

"So you hate dancing, too, do you?" he asked.

As he sat down next to me he exuded moroseness. It didn't worry me. In these grindingly positive times, I find the company of melancholics refreshing.

"I'd like it more if I was fitter," I replied.

We fell into mutual silence. Fear of sadness has become a global phobia. The moment someone is unhappy, people send them off to get antidepressants instead of sitting down and talking to them, which in many cases, is probably all they need. Without sadness, life would be flat and superficial like a roadside billboard. It would become impossible to appreciate joy. Besides, every great artist has found inspiration in pools of sorrow.

"Where are you from?" he asked.

I told him.

"I'm from the Upper West Side," he said. "My ancestors were from Albania. Everyone in New York is from somewhere else."

I quaffed my nonalcoholic cordial as he unraveled the story of his life, a string of disastrous romances. During a lull in his monologue, he turned his mournful face toward me and asked my marital status.

"*Twenty-two* years!" he said in a tone that implied I'd confessed to keeping a basement full of sex slaves. "How can anyone be married twenty-two years?"

I didn't like to say it was a question I'd been pondering, and that I was taking a sabbatical from my own marriage to figure out the answer. Instead, I told him the basis of a long marriage is about hoping the other person forgives your faults. In return, you try to overlook theirs.

"That wouldn't suit me," he said, shaking his head.

I agreed it wasn't for everyone.

"I want one hundred percent passion, sex, and romance," he said, warming to his theme. "For it to just fade into the two of you staring at your phones over the dinner table . . ."

He threw up a hand in disgust. The man had a point. As Michaela and Gene spun past, locked in each other's gaze, it occurred to me that perhaps they had the ideal relationship. Though they lived in separate apartment buildings, they'd been together for fifteen years. In their case, it seemed a little personal space kept the oxygen flowing through their romance.

"Wanna know what my problem is?" he said, not waiting for an answer. "I'm lonely."

New York's a loner magnet. I'd heard some people go to live there specifically because they crave solitude. They're convinced they can live

184

more quietly on an island crammed with 72,000 people per square mile than one populated by a single coconut tree. Still, there's a difference between being alone and loneliness. Personally, I could think of nothing more appealing than being alone and free in this dazzling city.

"Everyone's alone to some extent," I said. "Even if you meet your soul mate and spend blissful decades together, one of you has to die first."

He didn't seem convinced.

"Besides, when you love someone you're always putting them first," I added. "When my mother was dying of cancer she spent her time reassuring the rest of us she wasn't in pain and everything was going to be okay."

"Guess it took her mind off things," he said.

"Sex and passion's fine, but there's only one person you'll go to bed with every night of your life," I said.

"Yeah, I've heard that one."

"It's a good insurance policy," I said. "If nobody else warms to us, we can at least like ourselves."

"But I *do* love someone," he said. "Wanna know who that is?"

There was no need to answer because he was going to tell me anyway.

"My dog."

I was immensely relieved. I took his happy

185

confession as confirmation he wasn't trying to pick me up. Also, the fact he had the sensitivity and wisdom to appreciate the love of an animal meant he was probably going to be okay.

"She has the most amazing personality," he went on. "We go for walks twice a day, and she's always waiting for me when I come home. She has this funny, sad face. When my uncle died last year she just *knew* it. She slept on my bed every night. She'd do anything for me . . ."

I patted the man's hand and said how happy I was for him. Then it was back to the dance floor for another round of do-si-dos, swings, and allemandes. I loved dancing with happy strangers who were no longer strange at all. Accepted and yet alone in a primal soup was exactly where I needed to be. And yet, I wondered how long the elation was going to last . . .

A couple of hours later, after we arrived back at the apartment, I inspected Bono's food bowl. The chicken had been licked clean away, but the pill lay on its side, alone and dateless.

*Chapter Sixteen*

# BRINKMANSHIP AT BERGDORF'S

*Cats and luxury
understand each other.*

Once or twice I sat down to write the blog, but there didn't seem much point. The minute I'd waved Lydia off in three days' time, I'd be returning our houseguest to Bideawee. Much as I'd hoped he'd warm to me, Bono narrowed his eyes and scurried away whenever he saw me. He still hadn't forgiven me for the pill episode.

I was going to miss Lydia terribly. Maybe my friends back home were right and I'd lost my senses thinking I could undergo reinvention in New York. Alluring as the city was, life here wasn't quite real.

When I was given the cancer diagnosis, the fear wasn't so much that I might be dying but that I hadn't fully lived. Could it be the aspects I liked least about my life back home were the things I needed most? Without Philip, Jonah, and our humdrum existence, the days had lost their steady beat. There was no one to share a history with, no foundation for the present. If I dropped dead on Fifth Avenue, an ambulance would show up. But nobody would care.

Still, I wasn't about to book a flight home and beg forgiveness. Staying on wasn't going to be straightforward, either. I'd have to find another apartment after the month's lease had run out.

"Isn't he adorable?!" Lydia said as Bono padded out from under the bed and rubbed against her leg.

"Yes," I said, "but he hasn't done number two in days."

Obsessing over Bono's bowels was my compensation for unrequited affection.

"He chomps through that chicken," Lydia said, as the cat sprang on her lap and allowed her to run her hand over his back. I felt a stab of jealousy.

"I know," I said. "I can't fathom how so much food can go in one end and not come out the other."

Bono gazed up at Lydia as if she were his personal goddess. I could tell he had a tender heart. She buried her nose in his fluffy mane.

"Oh, Bono!" she said in her special Bono voice. "I'm going to miss you so much!"

He mewed back at her, dropped to the floor, and padded after her toward the fridge. Since we'd started feeding him chicken, he'd developed a healthy devotion to the appliance. At some stage in his mysterious life, someone must have loved him, and he'd returned that affection.

Meantime, I was desperate to find a way of getting a pill into him. Down at the pet supply shop, Bluebell's coat glistened as she preened herself in the window. Doris waved from inside and beckoned us in.

"I've been thinking about you," she said. "How's it going with your foster cat?"

"Bono's lovely!" Lydia said. "He has the cutest haircut and such a sweet nature. You'd adore him, Doris."

"He has kidney failure," I added.

Concern flashed across Doris's face.

"How bad is it?" she asked.

"They've told us it's quite advanced."

"Don't worry," Doris said. "Every cat I owned had kidney failure. With good care they can go on for years. Magnolia lived with it for ten years till she was seventeen."

Bluebell sprang onto the counter.

"That's just it," I said. "Bono won't take his medication. He has a pill phobia."

"You're using the pill pouches?" Doris asked, running her hand over Bluebell's back.

"What's that?"

"They don't have pill pouches where you come from?" Doris asked, scandalized.

If they did I'd never heard of them.

"See here," she said, pointing at a poster on the wall behind her. "The pouches are made of special treat food. All you have to do is hide a pill inside them and the cat eats the whole thing."

I knew about that special treat stuff. Back home, lumps of it were sold in brightly colored plastic bags. I'd had to stop buying it because it was cocaine to Jonah. Still, I was willing to try anything.

We thanked Doris and hurried back to the apartment to set up a special treat pill pouch snare. Confident Bono's problem was solved, we waved him good-bye and succumbed to the irresistible call of the city.

Lydia's fascination with consumerism was far from over. I found Saks Fifth Avenue overwhelming so we headed toward Central Park and what looked like a more traditional, low-key department store. A little ignorance can be a good thing. If I'd known about Bergdorf Goodman, I'd have probably steered clear.

The place oozed more luxury than a panther's paw. Upstairs, I ogled the children's clothing.

"Look at this gorgeous little dress!" I said. "It's perfect for Annie. And it's only $10. Don't you love stores that combine quality with good pricing?"

Lydia bent over the price tag and pointed out that I'd misread the arrangement of zeros.

"It's actually $1,000," she said, taking it out of my hands and placing it back on the hanger.

A blond thirtysomething woman in a cashmere coat elbowed me aside.

"I really can't decide," she said to her impeccably groomed friend. "Gucci or Burberry for Samantha's baby shower?"

The woman held up two tiny vests, identical in size and color.

"Burberry's classic," the friend said. "But Gucci has that European style."

A dark line appeared between the blond woman's eyebrows. It must have been overlooked in her last botox appointment. Not since the invasion of Iraq had a decision carried so much weight.

"I know!" she said after a lengthy pause. "I'll take them both."

With her new outfit and hairdo, Lydia almost blended into the surroundings. But my wild hair and paint-spattered coat made me feel like a mongrel at a dog show. I was nowhere near skinny, tailored, and blow dried enough. However, like all the best-bred people, the sales staff went out of their way to put outsiders at ease.

We followed our noses down an escalator to a cosmetics department in the basement to find the entrance to what seemed a delightful little café. It was lunchtime and the prices on the menu board weren't outrageous.

"Excuse me, madam."

The voice belonged to a young man with luminous eyes. I was momentarily mesmerized by his dark suit and stylish hair. Until, to my horror, I saw he was wielding a large makeup brush.

"Would madam like a little touch-up before dining?" he asked.

Back home offering to touch someone up could land you in court.

"Not just now, thanks," I said, assuming the phrase had a different meaning in the States.

"Do you think we should leave?" I whispered to Lydia.

I tried to drag her away, but she stood her ground. A helpful waiter slid me out of my coat and pointed us to a corner banquette.

I lowered my backside onto the upholstery and pretended to study the menu. The place was unpretentious in an upmarket way. Well-dressed women picked birdishly at their salads.

"Is that mink?" Lydia asked, watching the waiter ferry another customer's coat to the cloak-room.

While I was uncomfortable amid all the understated privilege, she didn't seem at all intimidated.

"This is the sort of place a mother and daughter would plan a wedding in the Hamptons, don't you think?" she said.

I could hardly believe she of the Buddhist robes could adapt seamlessly to such opulent surroundings.

The waiter was reassuringly unsnooty as I tried to upscale my accent.

"Let's have a glass of wine," Lydia said.

"With *alcohol?*"

"You probably don't know, but in my early student days I got drunk most lunchtimes," she said.

The waiter smiled and suggested a light chardonnay with a hint of citrus.

"Wasn't that a chess club you used to go to?"

"That's what we *called* it," she said, flicking her hair. The new blond streaks made her look like a movie star. And was that a shimmer of lip gloss?

Two glasses appeared in front of us.

"Guess I learn something every day," I said. "Here's to a safe trip home."

"And to Bono," Lydia said, clinking my glass. "Oh, and there's something I want to talk to you about."

"A wedding in the Hamptons?" I asked.

"No," she laughed. "I know you're planning on taking him back to the shelter the minute I've gone."

"What makes you think that?"

"If you were serious about keeping him you'd have started the blog by now."

The waiter lowered our perfect salads onto the table.

"This is like visiting Buckingham Palace and having the queen make you pancakes," I whispered.

Lydia fixed me with her psychologist's gaze.

"Stop changing the subject," she said.

"Look, I like Bono, but he loathes me. It'll be like a bad marriage."

"He's the most beautiful little cat in the world," she said.

"I know, but I've spent a lifetime looking after helpless creatures. I've got caregiver's fatigue."

My daughter wasn't impressed.

"Things don't always work out, you know," I said. "What if I can't find him a home? If he dies because I can't get a pill inside him? It'll be heartbreaking."

Lydia raised a fork and sank it into her salad.

"If you can't do it for him, do it for me," she said. "Please, Mum. Promise?"

Music wafted from a speaker somewhere while I stared into my glass and tried to examine my options. There weren't any.

"Okay," I said. "I promise."

We hurried back to the apartment to see how the special treat pouches had gone down. Bono hadn't touched them. He'd ignored the chicken, too.

*Chapter Seventeen*

# TEARING MY HAIR OUT

*Cats are
people, too.*

Bono still looked like a famine victim. His coat was duller than ever. I worried his health was failing under our haphazard care. I'd been hoping he'd soon be in the arms of his caregivers at Bideawee in the next day or so. Jon and his helpers were far more capable of ministering the medication he needed. But Lydia had put an end to all that. If Bono was to survive with me, I'd need a new, workable regime.

I rang the shelter. A woman answered the phone.

"Is Jon there?"

"I'm sorry, he's out today. Can I help you?"

*Out?* How could a cat whisperer take a vacation?

"It's Bono," I said. "The little black cat with the . . ."

"We all know Bono," she said with a smile in her voice.

There was a shuffling sound under my bed. Bono was listening to every word.

"Well, I'm worried about him. He refuses to take a pill. I've tried everything."

"Is he drinking?" she asked.

"Yes. But he hasn't done number two. And he's so skinny."

I waited for the nice woman to tell me to return him immediately.

"He's always been a fussy eater," she said. "There's medication in the canned food we gave you."

"He doesn't like that much, either."

"Is he eating any of it?" she asked.

"A little, now and then."

"Well, that should be enough to keep him stable."

"What about the chicken?"

"If he doesn't like that anymore, you could try fresh fish."

I remembered Olivia once telling me wild cats demand more variety in their diets than domestic felines. If a street cat has a slice of rat fillet here, a chomp of cockroach there, he's likely getting all the nutrients he needs. A kitchen cat, by comparison, may have all her nutritional requirements met in a single can (or pile of dried food). I wondered if Bono's pickiness was more to do with his homeless days than his illness.

"When will Jon be back?" I asked.

"In a couple of days. Meantime, just relax and enjoy Bono. He's a great little cat."

Relax? With sole responsibility for a seriously ill cat?

Lydia would be with me for just two more days. I decided it was time to drag her to my personal mecca—Broadway. I wanted her to love musicals as much as I did. When I was growing up in small town New Zealand, musicals were my religion. I soaked up amateur productions of *South Pacific* and *The King and I* along with the milk from our local dairy farms. To me, Rodgers and Hammerstein were philosophers who understood everything about love, life, and death. In *Oklahoma!* they even showed they knew what it was like to live in a tiny community on the edge of the Earth. I adored musicals because they affirmed that all a spirited girl had to do was fall in love, get married, and live happily ever after.

To visit the birthplace of these works and walk the same streets as Gene Kelly, Julie Andrews, and Hugh Jackman was living the dream.

"Just think," I said, slipping my arm through hers. "We're breathing the same air as Sondheim!"

I might as well have said we'd be having toast for breakfast. It was an odd reversal of our roles when I visited her in her Sri Lankan monastery. Perhaps this was karmic payback for not understanding the thrill of meditating for twelve hours in 100 percent humidity inside a sweltering temple frequented by scorpions.

Sitting inside the Eugene O'Neill Theatre waiting for the curtain to rise on *The Book of Mormon*, my excitement was, I think, almost too much for her. Perhaps she was uncomfortable with the musical's theme of young, naive white people inflicting their religion on African villagers. But even she laughed out loud in the opening act when an actor dragged a dead donkey across the stage. No doubt it resonated with her experiences in the third world.

However, while I loved everything about *The Book of Mormon*, Lydia seemed to merely tolerate it. How she had missed out on the family musical theater gene remains a mystery. Her grandmother had starred as Katisha in three (admittedly amateur) productions of *The Mikado*. I couldn't believe there was not a hint of greasepaint in Lydia's veins. I guess some people just cannot get the hang of actors erupting into song every five minutes.

"Didn't you love it?!" I asked as we made our way out of the theater.

Her answer was short and muffled. It sounded like "quite".

On our way back to the apartment, she pointed out a poster for a play by Norah Ephron also running on Broadway. *Lucky Guy* was Ephron's last play. Starring Tom Hanks, it was about a newspaper columnist living in New York in the 1980s. I wanted her last night to be one to remember. If I couldn't change her mind about musicals, I thought she might at least enjoy a play. Miraculously, seats were still available. I booked two for tomorrow, her last night in town.

Bono was in his usual position under the bed when we opened the door to the apartment. A resident rat would have been friendlier.

While she was in the shower, I opened my laptop. After a few watery bleeps, Philip appeared on the screen. He was sitting in front of the fire with a blanket and Jonah draped over his knee.

"What have you been up to?" he asked.

"Not much. We've just been to *The Book of Mormon*. It was fantastic. You'd love it. And we went shopping. Lydia bought this fabulous handbag and . . ." I needed to play down how much fun we'd been having. "How's work?"

"Hectic as usual. We had to let someone go."

I knew how much he hated doing that. Through the years, I'd learned the corporate world is a shark tank, eat or be eaten.

"Sorry about that," I said.

He looked older than I remembered. I was older too, of course, but only on the outside. Jonah blinked at me and yawned.

"It's freezing here," he said. "We've got to sort the heating out before winter."

I'd forgotten how our house was an oven in the summer and a refrigerator by the time autumn came along. It didn't seem fair to tell him about daffodils in Central Park, and the thermometer climbing by the day.

"How's that cat?" he asked.

"Bono? He's a handful. How's our boy?"

"He's been licking his fur too much. He's almost bald down one leg. See?"

Philip held up Jonah's front leg to show me a pale strip down the side of it. Jonah flicked me a pitiful look.

"Has that gray cat been bullying him again? Are you remembering his pill?" I asked.

"The vet thinks it's separation anxiety. She says to give him as much attention as I can."

"Really?" I said, swallowing hard. Poor Jonah. To be honest, with all the worry about Bono, I'd hardly thought of him. Still, Jonah was in good hands.

"Where do we keep the sheets?" he asked.

"In the laundry cupboard."

"They're all too small for our bed."

"Just sort through them," I said. "Try the green ones."

I was almost relieved after they melted into the dark screen. I wasn't about to hurry home to go on a sheet safari. Still, I felt guilty about Jonah. Since the cancer episode, I'd made a point of saying yes to life. But that Skype session had left me feeling more than a little selfish.

I wondered if showing me Jonah's leg had been Philip's way of telling me he needed me, too. If he hadn't mentioned the sheets, I might have been tempted to fly home.

On the other hand, there was so much I'd missed out on through four decades of mothering.

I'd spent the last years of my childhood in the 1970s giving birth and raising two small boys, Sam and Rob. The 1980s were consumed with grief after Sam's death, followed by the joy of Lydia's birth. The 1990s were about remarriage and giving birth again, this time to Katharine. Through all those phases, I never stopped working, writing for newspapers, magazines, and television. Occasionally, it seemed things had not really happened until I'd made sense of them on paper, and later a computer screen. If I could not find out who I was and complete myself now, in my late fifties, when would I?

Back in Melbourne, all the days seemed the same. Weeks drifted into years. In New York, every moment was etched with intensity. Lying under the purple curtains each night, I would brim with childish excitement for the next day.

Much as I loved Philip, I wasn't sure I could ever shrink myself down to fit into our old routine in front of the fire again. My parents had spent their sunset years like that, and Mum became bitter about the compromises she'd made. She'd practically died with a tea tray in her hands. I did not know how I wanted to end up, but it was not like that.

After you've fallen in love and burst into song a few times, the business of real life begins. There are not many musicals about childbirth, trash nights, and whose turn it is to do the dishes. It's a shame Rodgers and Hammerstein never wrote about that part.

Once Lydia had returned to Australia, nobody would care if I hummed along with the cast at musicals or made an idiot of myself pretending to be a native New Yorker. Of course, I'd honor my promise to look after Bono a while longer and start the blog. But even if a thousand people read it, he was bound to end up back at Bideawee. Once that happened I'd no longer need to fret over anyone's emotional development or if they'd done number two.

Like a glorious Persian rug, a life of limitless possibilities lay before me.

## Chapter Eighteen

# STARSTRUCK

*A cat prefers
to be adored.*

When I move to New York, I'll live in walking distance of Broadway and see every show. I love how the theaters are so small and old-fashioned. The smell of dust and disinfectant is a reminder the greatest dreams are built on muck and microbes.

The only thing not to like is the intermission stampede for the restrooms. Something's out of whack when it's possible to print 3D versions of the heart, yet there still aren't enough bathrooms for women in theaters.

*Lucky Guy* was fantastic. As the actors took their bows at the end, I stood and clapped until my hands were numb.

"What did you think?" Lydia asked, as we joined the throng of people surging into the theater foyer.

"Tom Hanks is amazing," I said. "Some actors can't make the transition from television to a theater stage, but I couldn't take my eyes off him."

Lydia hugged her program and smiled.

"Did you like it more than *The Book of Mormon*?" she asked.

How could I not? In his role as tabloid journalist Mike McAlary, Tom Hanks had practically stepped out of my past.

"Newsrooms were tough for women back in the

seventies and eighties," I said, digging my hands in my pockets. "The guys we worked with would be in jail these days."

I told her how in my first week as a cadet reporter, aged 18, the chief reporter took me to a bar and announced he was going to have his way with me in the back of his car.

"What did you do?" she asked.

"I was young and naive enough to laugh in his face."

Norah Ephron had clearly endured similar experiences during the same era in New York, and crafted them into art.

"Do you think he's still here?" Lydia asked.

"Who, Tom? He's probably backstage taking his makeup off. We might see him if we wait at the stage door."

"Really?"

"He has to get out of the building somehow. He might even sign your program," I said, handing her a pen.

We were disappointed to see the stage door clogged with fans, so we crossed the street to observe from a distance. There was a group gasp as an imposing silhouette emerged. Hundreds of smartphones raised in unison. We watched enviously as the star stopped to chat with people and sign their programs.

"He must have been wearing a wig on stage," Lydia said.

I removed my glasses and wiped them on my coat sleeve. She was right. The actor was as bald as a barracuda.

"That's not Tom!" I said, squinting my eyes. "It's that other actor. You know, the old guy."

We watched him vanish into the crowd to become anonymous as the rest of us.

We waited . . . and waited. Tom would surely have wiped his makeup off by now. The crowd outside the theater was peaceful, but it was growing larger. A restless ripple ran through them. I turned to see a dozen or so mounted police lining up at the end of the street.

These were not cuddly ponies that could be disarmed with the offering of a carrot. The horses were immensely tall. To a Tom Hanks disciple with a dodgy knee they were downright intimidating. White clouds snorted out of their nostrils and hovered on the cold night air. A riot shield reflected the flash of a neon sign.

"Let's go," I said.

But Lydia pretended not to hear. I watched in alarm as she crossed the street to join the knot of hardcore fans outside the stage door. I called after her, but she was in a trance. I leaned against a post and tried to enjoy the spectacle. Every time a figure appeared from inside the theater, the crowd inhaled a single breath—only to release a sigh when they realized it wasn't Tom but another actor eager to sprinkle his charm over them like glitter.

By now, I was pretty sure Tom had taken the back exit and was soaking in the Jacuzzi at his hotel. To my horror, the row of horses started to march down the street toward us, their heads bowed as if they were trying to remember what was on their shopping lists.

People dispersed. I couldn't decide if I should run across the street to find Lydia, or keep walking back along my side of the sidewalk, in the hope she'd find me later. A gush of maternal instinct took over and, suffragette style, I dashed in front of the glistening hooves. Heart throbbing behind my eyes, I grabbed her elbow and steered her toward a quieter part of town.

"I wanted to bring you somewhere special for your last night," I said as we stopped outside a discreet-looking building on West 44th Street.

"I don't like jazz," she said

I begged her to approach Birdland with an open mind. Named after Charlie Parker, the alto sax magician known as "Bird," the club has earned its reputation as jazz corner of the world.

The moment we entered the dark crimson interior, I felt christened with cool. We sat at a small table and ordered drinks while a quartet poured notes of molten gold in our ears.

From the corner of my eye, I watched as Lydia's expression changed from not liking jazz to liking it very much indeed. Her attention was focused on the African American pianist who was playing as if he had four sets of hands. After he ripped into an improvised solo, she clapped furiously. My daughter was infatuated.

Love has many facets. Falling hard and fast for a jazz pianist can be just as powerful as other manifestations. After the show, the pianist sat dining alone at the bar.

"Why don't you go and say hello to him?" I asked.

Lydia seemed mortified at the idea.

"It's the last thing he wants," she said.

"He's an artist. Someone like him thrives on people's admiration. For him it's oxygen."

She refused to budge, but her eyes were glued to him.

"What would I say to him?" she asked.

"Just tell him how much you enjoyed the show. It'll make his night."

We gathered our coats. As I was settling the bill, she overcame her reticence and strode toward the musician. He looked up and offered her a seat. Their heads bent toward each other as they exchanged words. The man gazed down at his chest and said something that made Lydia laugh. They were so engaged in the timeless art of flirting, I wondered if I should make excuses and leave.

But a few minutes later, Lydia stood up and joined me at the door. As we walked back to the apartment through the freezing night, she was flushed and elated.

"What are you thinking?" I asked.

Not so long ago, I wouldn't have dared ask such a prying question. If I had, she would have retreated like a shellfish.

"I'm thinking," she said, gazing up at the glittering towers. "That one day I'm going to have a rescue cat."

I pictured Lydia and Ramon with a cat draped over their laps. Who knows what that would lead to? A pet, then a baby. If that happened, they could bring it to visit me once or twice a year.

In between times, I could sing Broadway songs to it over Skype.

Because what woman in her right mind would turn down the chance to live in New York?

## Chapter Nineteen

# FUR-FILLING A PROMISE

*There's no better companion
for a writer than a cat.*

Lydia stood in the middle of our apartment clutching the sheets she'd slept between for the past ten days. She handed them to me in a bundle and asked if I'd mind bringing the blanket we had bought back with me when I returned to Australia. There was not room for it in her backpack and she'd grown attached to it. With her bed flipped back to a sofa again, the room seemed sharp edged and clinical. I could hardly believe she was going. I asked if she wanted to take any of the art gallery postcards from the mantelpiece. She tucked Monet's water lilies—her water lilies, from now on—in a pocket of her backpack.

New York had transformed our relationship. We were accepting our differences without leaping to conclusions, taking risks, and laughing together. I was amazed at how the city had opened her eyes to art, fashion, jazz, and theater. After her years of religious modesty, the city had unlocked her sensuality. From shopping at Victoria's Secret to chatting up a jazz pianist, she'd succumbed to the ambient vibrancy and allowed herself to flourish.

More important, I'd never seen her open her heart so willingly to a living creature.

"Oh, and this is for Bono," she said, reaching into her pack and handing me a cat fishing rod. "Don't forget to play with him."

Sensing something was up, the cat trotted out from under the bed and rubbed against her legs. Though he refused to let her pick him up, as usual, he invited her to run her hand over his back.

"Oh, Bono!" she said, tears cascading down her cheeks. "I'm going to miss you so much."

He fixed her with his golden gaze and nuzzled her fingers.

"You will find him a home, won't you?" she asked, taking a tissue from her sleeve.

As a parent, it doesn't matter how old your child is. Whether they're 4 or 40, you'd remove your own appendix with a kitchen knife if it helped heal your child's pain.

"I'll do my best," I said, leading her downstairs and out to the street.

For once, we didn't have to wait for a cab.

"We had a good time, didn't we?" I said, giving her a hug. Though I never like saying good-bye to my kids, I always try to orchestrate the occasion to be pleasant, in case life takes one of its horrendous twists and it turns out to be the final farewell.

"Look after Bono, won't you?" she said. "I can't wait to read the first blog."

She was still crying as she climbed into the backseat.

I went upstairs. Bono was back in his hiding place. The room felt empty without Lydia.

Being alone in New York was going to be more challenging than I'd imagined. I felt vulnerable, unwanted, and past my best before date—like a sick cat without a home. A pair of amber headlights beamed out at me from under the bed. He didn't like me. Come to think of it, he wasn't the cat I would have chosen, either. But Lydia loved him, and he had spirit. Maybe the cat and I could prop each other up and create a new life together. If nothing else, he'd be someone to come home to.

"What do you think, Bono? You, me, and the big smoke. Shall we give it a try?"

The headlights blinked.

I slid my laptop out of its case, placed it on the little table beside the fireplace. Not for the first time, I wondered why so many people think they want to be writers. For workplace companionship it's the equivalent of lighthouse keeping. When working on a book, I'm lucky to have more than one human interaction a day, usually with a barista. Once my recyclable cup is filled with the required fix, I scurry home to stare at the vacant computer screen. That's when I invent excuses not to write, such as cleaning out the fridge, emptying the dishwasher, or going to the bathroom.

Writing is more tiring than people think. I've

usually run out of steam by lunchtime, so I'll lie on the bed and drift to sleep listening to a recorded meditation. After that, I watch daytime TV with the windows shut in case our next-door neighbor, Heather, hears.

My work is usually at its worst on days when words flow and I think I'm on a roll. The best sentences emerge childlike in their simplicity after countless times through the rinse cycle.

At night, I go to sleep reworking the day's paragraphs inside my head. A lot of the ideas seem brilliant, but I've usually forgotten them by morning.

Friendships go on hold. After a few months, I forget how to hold a conversation. When the book finally emerges and needs promotion, I'm expected to undergo a personality change to become witty, well-dressed, and outgoing.

For all its challenges, an author's life has expanded my world in ways I would never have imagined. No doubt the contrast between emptying garbage at home and being treated like royalty in an Austrian castle or strolling the shores of Lake Como with my Italian translator had contributed to my restlessness.

At book fairs and on tour in various countries there were encounters that will stay with me a lifetime—the woman in Warsaw who stood up and said through an interpreter that our family was Poland's family; in Japan weeping with tsunami victims who simply wanted to express their pain. I'll never forget giving a reading in Vienna in an exquisite room where Mozart had performed, or meeting high school students in Portugal to learn they faced the same challenges as Australian teenagers. Wherever I go I meet people whose animal guardians have helped them through loss and pain.

The emails are often deeply moving, too. I try to respond to them all. Every now and then, a reader travels across the globe to meet Jonah. He has received guests from Italy, Canada, Switzerland, and France. They've all been women with a happy blend of intelligence and charm. While Jonah holds court, I serve homemade banana cake, which seems a trifle considering how far they've traveled.

The machine hummed to life and the screen lit up with an expectant air. I drew a breath and typed *"Huffington Post* Blog." Headings are always easy. Two coffees and a fruit tart later, I raised my fingers to the keyboard again.

*Bono was the strangest looking cat I'd ever seen . . .*

### Chapter Twenty

# BROKEN WINDOW, OPEN HEART

*A woman's best
bodyguard is her cat.*

I finished the first blog post and pressed send. Though words can be powerful and enduring, I wasn't confident they'd be enough to change the life of my four-legged lodger. No matter how much I played down his illness and how appealing I made him seem, the notion of a *Huffington Post* reader wanting to adopt him was nothing short of fanciful.

With my newfound freedom, it was time to get out and among it. If the buzz of the city couldn't lift my mood, nothing would.

Since trading in my boots for a pair of running shoes with marshmallow soles, I'd started to appreciate walking. Like most New Yorkers, I was probably averaging four miles a day, but the sidewalks were hard on my feet. Even if I owned a thousand pairs of shoes in this city I'd still end up wearing soft-cushioned sneakers every day.

I clomped down the hill toward Grand Central Station and stopped outside the dress shop Lydia had loved so much. There was no point going inside to look at clothes that didn't suit or fit me.

I needed to be around people, so I headed to Times Square. The Naked Cowboy tipped his hat. He wasn't technically nude, but there was still a mountain of flesh on display. I remember how amused Lydia had been by his strategically placed guitar. I stood under the National Debt Clock and watched the numbers spin at a dizzying pace. The clock seemed to be warning that everyone's lives were flicking away at great speed and it was about time we took notice. Times Square used to be fun when Lydia was here. Now it was just crowded and tawdry.

The blazing neon signs hurt my eyes. A hawker in a matted Elmo outfit pestered me to pose for a photo with him. After I sent him away, he wandered off to a bench, took his head off, and lit a cigarette. The man under the Elmo mask looked so disillusioned and exhausted, I went over and tossed him some coffee money.

From Times Square I escaped to the relative sanctuary of the diner where Lydia and I had shared our first meal. Without her, I felt vulnerable trying to keep pace with the tide of humanity, at the same time fighting my antipodean tendency to veer left.

Maybe I'd taken on this adventure thirty years too late. What if I fell over, dropped my wallet, or lost my passport? Getting mugged didn't worry me so much. Out on the street, I was a single blood cell pulsing through a vein—too anonymous to be singled out for attack. Besides, there was no sense in worrying about something beyond my control.

"S'cuse me, Ma'am," a male voice said as I paused to cross at a red light. "Your shoelace is undone."

It was a casual act of kindness but it cheered me up. Perhaps New York would one day feel like home to this stranger from another land.

Yet I was feeling the achy pull of my old life. The leaves on the tree in our back garden would be turning yellow and starting to drop. Jonah would be curled in front of the fire, and with any luck had stopped licking his leg. I needed to tell Philip how I missed the warmth of his body and holding hands on our Sunday morning walks. Back at the apartment, when I set up the laptop for Skype, I was shocked at how ancient I looked on screen. I pulled the curtain to soften the light and positioned the computer at an angle that disguised my scraggy neck. I meant to start on a romantic note. Instead, my voice had a querulous edge.

"Where is he?" I asked, when Philip appeared.

Though he smiled and seemed pleased to see me, I could tell his attention was elsewhere.

"Who, Jonah? Asleep upstairs, I think."

"How's that patch on his leg?"

"Oh, the same, maybe a bit worse."

"*Worse?!* How worse?"

"He's okay."

I recognized that offhand lack of engagement in my husband.

"You're watching rugby, aren't you?"

His eyes drifted sideways. Some meaty-thighed player must have kicked a goal.

"I'd better not keep you," I said.

He accepted my offer almost too readily. With his rugby and his glass of beer, he seemed to be enjoying life rather too much without me.

"I suppose it's only natural after twenty-two years a man would rather watch rugby," I said, closing the laptop.

This wasn't good. I was talking to myself. Then I remembered what Jon had said about reading to kittens. Just the sound of a human voice can make a difference. So, I addressed the invisible lodger lurking under the bed.

"Gosh, Bono, my knee hurts. Is that why you do those arabesques with your back leg? Have you got arthritis or something? Do you think you could ever like me? I don't eat cats, you know. Besides, neither of us is in our prime. Which reminds me, it would be very good if you could have a go at doing number two sometime. What do you think, Bono?"

My questions were answered with silence. I closed my eyes and tried to tune into my furry housemate on a psychic wavelength. The words that bounced into my head were loud and clear—
*"You're crazy!"*

As the light faded, I walked to a neighborhood bar where an amiable group of people was engrossed in a basketball game on the television above the bartender's head. They erupted into cheers every now and then. Though I've tried to understand rugby for the sake of our marriage, the allure of sport remains a mystery. I can appreciate the athletes' fine young bodies and the discipline it takes to acquire them, but whatever game they're playing it's nothing beyond stylized warfare. I glanced at the intense faces smiling over their beers—and felt profoundly alone.

Later, back at the apartment, I slid all the locks across the inside of our front door. Reassured I was safely shut away from the world, I checked the windows. To my dismay, the window lock above my bed was completely broken. Through all the time Lydia and I had been living there, someone could have climbed the fire escape and let himself in.

There was no point phoning Ted or whoever was manning the rental agency. I'd only get an answering machine at this hour. Philip would be fast asleep with Jonah between his knees. What could he do from this distance, anyway? Calling the cops would be melodramatic under the circumstances. There was no one to turn to. Chilled with fear, I closed the curtains, turned the light off, and climbed into bed. Thanks to city lights filtering through the purple curtains, the darkest our apartment ever got was a dusky mauve. I pulled Lydia's blanket over my face, clutched my pillow, and longed to be back home in front of the fire.

While I was willing sleep to transport me to a friendlier, safer place, something jumped on the bed. Rigid with fright, I fought the urge to scream.

Seconds later, to my great relief, I watched the silhouette of a tiny black lion bounce over the covers to nestle beside my feet.

*Chapter Twenty-one*

# ALONE,
# NOT LONELY

*A feline sees beauty
in every day.*

I woke the next morning with a pompom in my face. As my eyes cleared, it became clear it was not a pompom, but the fluffy tip of Bono's tail. He was curled up on the pillow next to mine. His owlish eyes fixed me with an unblinking stare.

Repressing the urge to cry out and throw grateful arms around him, I closed my eyes again and pretended to sleep. After what seemed several lifetimes, I felt something flicking leisurely across my nostrils. Bono was using his tail as my wake-up call.

Much as I longed to reach out and run my hands through his scruffy mane, the cat had made it clear what the dynamics of our relationship were. He was the rock star, and I was the humble fan.

"Good morning sir," I said. "How long have you been sitting there?"

He blinked and dipped his head the way I'd seen him do with Lydia when inviting her attention. Smiling, I slowly raised a hand to scratch his forehead with my forefinger— anything more would have been presumptuous. I couldn't help noticing how flat and broad his head was compared to Jonah's.

As Bono raised his chin and allowed me to stroke his scraggy neck, he emitted something I hadn't heard before—a light but unmistakable purr. Compared to Jonah's throaty rumble, Bono's was a tinkling music box melody.

Without thinking, I sat up and reached out to stroke his back.

His fur was dull and wiry. The addition of fresh fish and chicken to his diet had done little to improve his coat. Bono sprang off the bed and flitted into the shadows underneath the mattress.

Though I missed Lydia, it seemed that her absence had allowed Bono to offer a tentative paw of friendship. And in the days that followed, I discovered it could be liberating to experience the city without the blur of another's wants and perceptions.

Wandering the streets of New York, I became reacquainted with someone I hadn't known for decades. She was older and less naive than the last time we hung out together. I didn't mind her company, and I learned some things I'd forgotten about her, too.

In a field of sunflowers, there's always one bloom facing a different direction from the others—not surrendering membership of the group, just taking a different perspective. That's her.

She was the person an overzealous store detective would decide to shadow because she hadn't paid neurotic attention to her looks. She wandered aimlessly about the store with her mind on other things, which the store detective interpreted as suspicious behavior. When she reached her hand into her pocket, the detective would approach to offer help. This would be pointless because unless he'd like to discuss the morning cloud formations and if he also thought they looked like nudes painted by Ingres, she wasn't interested.

When people were piling onto a bus or train, she was usually the last anyone sat next to. She didn't know why—perhaps it had to do with her size or her distracted expression. Perhaps she looked forbidding. Though she paid attention to how she dressed, she sometimes wondered if she was mistaken for a bag lady. She didn't care— she reckoned street people deserve more kudos than they get.

She was also the person in the wrong seat at the movie theater. It was quite usual for an outraged woman to accost her, and demand she get out of her seat. If the other woman was calm enough to inspect the tickets, usually they would discover she was in the right seat all along—but if that woman wanted it badly, she'd let her take it.

She had more than a passing acquaintance with grief. The fissures in her heart were permanent, but they were not a deformity. They were the spaces into which she could invite others who wanted to unburden their sadness. To share another's sorrow, whether it was a close friend or a reader from the other side of the world, was one of life's great privileges.

She liked silence. There was so much to hear in it.

If forced to choose, she'd be a cat rather than a dog. Not because she wrote about cats. Dogs were straightforward. They revealed everything about themselves in exchange for a bowl of meat. A cat, on the other hand, shared what it thought you should know, and reserved the right to disappear.

Flowers affected her. They were a reminder of the beauty and fragility of life. Whenever she carried a bunch along a street, whether it was in New York or Melbourne, cars would slow down to let her cross. A person with flowers was signaling themselves as a lover or a beloved. They could be caring for a troubled friend, or the focus of someone else's concern. With flowers in your arms, you walked in a halo of love.

People at the beginning and end of life interested her. She loved it when a baby stared up from his stroller and raised his chubby fingers in salute. Or when an old man's eyes blazed with recognition in exchange for a passing nod. Those on the edges appreciated the miracle of being here. Their priorities were straight. They savored every moment. Animals had a similar approach.

She liked watching the way a mother's lips open and close as she feeds small pieces of bread to her infant. The faces of small children were fascinating. Some were already middle-aged in expression. Familial similarities intrigued her. The way a set of ears or eyes gets carried through generations was fascinating.

Though she'd lost a child, a breast, a brother, parents, and a number of close friends, she didn't dwell on what life had taken from her. Life gave far more than it took away, and continued to do so every day.

In an age when so many people were fixated by the hyper real world inside their phones, she found the sight of lovers reassuring. It would be a long time before two robots fell in love with each other.

The danger, she felt, wasn't so much that robots were becoming people, but the other way around. Watching commuters on the subway, she was saddened by how everyone in the car lowered their head over a phone. Their eyes glazed over as they switched off and sank into states of semi-hypnosis. The last thing they touched at night was their cool sliver of technology. When they woke in the morning, the first thing they reached for wasn't the warmth of another human, but their phone. It made her wonder how long it took to forget how to be human—one generation, or two?

She understood why pets had surged in popularity. People needed the comfort of warm fur, the gleam of a trusting eye more than ever. In many cases, it was all they had to stay connected to their animal selves.

Though she relished the company of friends and family, she was equally content sitting alone in a diner listening to others try to make sense of their world.

That was the woman I came to know again. So, while I was alone in New York, I was far from lonely. I had myself for company, and I quite liked it.

I also had Bono. Whether I was bathing my senses in a Wagner opera at Lincoln Center or munching on pizza at Lombardi's in Nolita, I knew that on the third floor of a not very elegant building near the UN, a small beating heart was waiting for me.

One morning, as I rifled through my underwear in search of one of my new bras, I came across a furry pink cat toy I'd brought from Australia. I placed it on the floor beside the bed and went out for the day.

When I returned that evening, Bono was tossing the thing around the apartment as if it was the best pet toy that had ever been invented. And to my elation, he'd started doing number two.

## Chapter Twenty-two

# TELLING TALES

*To be granted permission
to stroke a cat is a high compliment.*

I'd heard nothing from the *Huffington Post* and was beginning to wonder whether they had even received my first blog. Concerned by the lack of response, I called Vida. She responded with her trademark breeziness saying she'd spoken to an editor there and it was going to take a few days for the blog to be posted. Next to Michaela, Vida was the biggest non-worrier I'd ever met.

Meantime, Vida added, the publishing house would like me to bring Bono along to the book launch they were hosting in ten days. It would be in a pet shop so Bono wouldn't be lonely.

I tried to explain that Bono hosting a book launch would be like Howard Hughes starring in his own song and dance spectacular. It would traumatize him, and undo the progress we'd made. If he was put on show in front of strangers, he'd curl up in a ball and have even less chance of finding a home.

In the end we agreed to make a decision closer to the time.

Even if for some reason *Huffington Post* decided not to use my stuff, I went ahead with a second blog post.

"I'm only trying to help you," I said to my

241

roommate, who remained gregarious as an Easter Island monument.

*No one said it was going to be easy . . .* I typed, like a schoolgirl telling tales. *Bono refused to budge from under the bed.*

As I hammered away, a set of whiskers appeared from the shadows. A nose and a set of traffic light eyes nudged forward. Watching me from the safety of his cave entrance, the cat seemed curious. I called his name, but he didn't respond.

"You are a high-maintenance, unrewarding animal," I said, turning my attention back to the keyboard. "And you can stay there as long as you like."

With half a blog under my belt, I flopped on the couch and flicked through the TV channels. In a strange variation of Stockholm syndrome, America's bitter struggle for freedom from Britain seemed to have left the nation obsessed with *Downton Abbey* and *Call the Midwife*. Though I was intrigued by their version of *Antiques Roadshow*, it soon anaesthetized me into a stupor. I was about to switch the thing off, when a tiny figure trotted across the room toward me.

I froze, and pretended to be fascinated by the commercials. Bono moved closer and nudged the edge of my shoe with his forehead. Resisting the urge to cry out and embrace him, I ignored him and kept staring at the TV. Bono emitted a bell-like mew. I pretended not to hear.

When he leapt on the sofa and sat beside me, my heart melted like the ice cream in our fridge that didn't work. I leaned toward him. He hesitated, as if he might change his mind and scurry for cover. But he stood still and he let me slide my hand over his bony spine.

The human hand is ideally shaped to stroke a cat's spine. The curves are designed to fit into one another. With a few more swishes, I could hear the hum of feline throat muscles vibrating. According to Olivia, a ten-year study at the University of Minnesota found that cat owners were 40 percent less likely to have heart attacks than people who didn't have live-in purr machines. As Bono's humming grew louder with every swish, I could feel my muscles relax, my lungs take in slower, deeper breaths.

As he raised his face, his eyes seared through to my soul. In him I saw the wildness of the magpie's gaze, the untouchable beauty of a creature who doesn't question his purpose, or fret over the fact his life is limited to a few short years.

Bono and I recognized something in each other. We were both adrift, a little knocked around and uncertain how the rest of our lives were going to pan out. We were lost and looking for something. Neither of us were sure where we belonged. Bono snared my heart in that moment. No matter how confusing everything around us was, we had each other.

"Don't you worry, my friend," I said. "I'll find you a home."

The touch of his fur made me realize I was homesick. And yet, as Bono rested his dainty paw on my lap and dipped his face in my hand, I knew the cat had claimed me. And so, in its way, had New York. Both of us were starting to feel we belonged. The city that never sleeps is in actual fact the city that never shuts up. Every morning before dawn I'd wake to the grind and clatter of construction against the ambient thrum of tires on asphalt. As the working day began, the hum of air-conditioning units would be punctuated by taxi horns, sirens, brakes squealing, and trucks backing up. Out on the sidewalks, the background hum of a hundred different languages would be interrupted by the unlikely sound of a police horse clearing its throat. Sometimes, the noise and energy of the city morphed into a monster that left me drained. The relief of retreating to our building and the comfort of sliding the key into the heart-shaped lock was immeasurable.

Every floor of our building had a slightly different aroma. Down at street level it was redolent of the vehicle fumes and cabbage. Up the first flight on the so-called second floor, the odor gave way to hints of overcooked pasta mingled with cheese.

I worried that our floor had a meaty overlay that betrayed the presence of our animal stowaway. My offhand exchanges with Ted had left me uncertain whether our apartment was officially pet friendly. If we were breaking some kind of communal code by having Bono, I worried the residents might appear bearing pitchforks at our door. After tracing a dank, sour smell that seemed to be emanating from the communal garbage chute, I was relieved to find an empty bag of kitty litter among the garbage. Until I realized it was ours.

Below us, the third floor reeked of cigarettes and socks. The inhabitants of the third floor seemed to communicate with each other solely through signage. Each brown door was embellished with a No Smoking notice, apart from the one directly below us. Whoever lived in there had retaliated with the DO NOT SLAM DOORS! banner. I'd studied that angry scribble at leisure because it was where I usually stopped to catch my breath on the way up.

After a successful day out buying clothes that both fitted and weren't black, I paused for the regulation breather on the third floor. To my astonishment, the DO NOT SLAM DOORS! sign moved. A pair of spectacles with lenses thick as latte glasses appeared from a crack in the door.

"Been shopping at a place for women of a certain age, have we?" said the owner of the spectacles in a heavy Irish accent.

His face was narrow and lined, the hair unnaturally dark against his pallid skin.

"How do you know?" I asked, taken aback.

"A friend of mine used to go out with her years ago," he said, nodding at a woman's name emblazoned across my shopping bag. "Her brand's very successful."

My indignant reaction gave way to amusement.

"Are you saying I should buy clothes from a different shop?" I asked, subconsciously scanning his outfit. With a gray cardigan sagging over an open-necked houndstooth shirt, he was hardly the personification of Karl Lagerfeld.

"Not at all," he said. "I'm saying it's a shop for older women."

Clothes are an ongoing source of anxiety for me. I'm always on the lookout for a self-appointed stylist.

"Do you mean her outfits are designed for someone older than me?"

"That depends," he said. "How old are you?"

The conversation was getting ridiculous. And now I was starting to worry he wasn't gay after all. Besides, when I was growing up, few things were more scandalous than mutton dressing as lamb. Surely it was appropriate for this side of hog to buy frocks from a shop for old sheep.

He introduced himself as Patrick. After he found out what I did for a living, he assured me he knew every great writer who'd ever lived in

New York. Arthur Miller was a moody sod, but Frank McCourt, who wrote *Angela's Ashes*, was his best friend. But Frank was dead now, of course. Every great writer seemed to be underground clutching his Remington typewriter.

Patrick asked if I had cockroaches. I said I hadn't seen any so far. He wanted to know how much a month I was paying. I told him I couldn't remember, which was true. Whatever it was it was bound to be too much, he said.

"And tell me, what is it you've written about?" he asked, pulling a cigarette from his pocket and fixing me with a froglike gaze.

"Um, a cat," I replied, humbled by the pedigree of his literary friends.

He sucked his cheeks in what I thought was an attempt to disguise disappointment.

"I see now. Would that be a children's book?"

When I explained it wasn't, and that the cat was a metaphor in some ways, he said he wouldn't mind reading it. I told him I'd drop a copy by sometime.

"Good," he said, lighting the cigarette and inhaling as if his life depended on it. "So, you'll be coming down for a cup of tea then."

Confused and vaguely annoyed, I toiled up the final flight of stairs clasping my new old-women's clothes. I made a point of slamming the door. Still, it was reassuring to know somebody in New York drank tea.

## Chapter Twenty-three

# BECOMING LOCAL

*A cat likes to belong,
yet retain her outsider status.*

Instead of having breakfast alone at home, I now ate at the deli across Second Avenue. The ambience of ordinary people getting ready for their working day was companionable. I liked scraping oatmeal into a paper cup and topping it with walnuts, berries, and an occasional blob of cream. The cappuccino wasn't bad, either.

When a cop in a UN uniform ordered his omelets in fluent Spanish, I suffered a pang of language envy. The chef cracked three eggs in a pan with expert ease and turned to me.

"You want turs?" he asked.

"Turs?" I asked, a prickle of discomfort crawling down my neck.

The cop looked down at me, amusement in his eye.

"Si," the chef said, leaning into my face and shouting. "Do you want turs or no!?"

I'd never heard of turs. Maybe it was some kind of taco.

"*Toast,*" the cop said, breaking into a smile. "He's saying toast."

Blushing, I glanced down at the weapon tucked into the cop's belt. Though he seemed friendly I'll never get used to policemen with guns. Still,

I couldn't help appreciating the solid lines of his shoulders as he ran a hand through his glossy dark hair.

"Thanks for helping me out," I said, as the chef passed him the omelet.

"My pleasure, ma'am. You're not from these parts?"

"No, but I'm having a wonderful time in your city," I said to avoid risking arrest more than anything else.

"New York!" he said, rolling his eyes. "I'm sick of this city."

"What do you mean?" I asked.

"It's boring."

I could imagine being wrung out from living in New York, or perhaps in his line of work, even battle worn. But to be bored of New York is surely to be bored with life.

"Where else do you want to live?" I asked.

"I can't wait to move to a log cabin."

I'd met people who lived in cabins, admittedly made of asbestos rather than log, and they were desperate to move out.

"Where would you find one of those?" I asked.

His eyes clouded with a dreamy look.

"In the mountains somewhere."

I didn't say anything to disillusion him, but he obviously hadn't tried living in a log cabin lately.

Though I was a foreigner, I no longer felt like a tourist. Like the people trotting behind their dogs along the sidewalks, I'd become a thread in the fabric of the city, an honorary citizen with an animal to go home to.

Locals like me had a different air. We didn't clutch maps and guidebooks or shuffle about missing everything worth seeing because we were fixated on the map inside our phone. Though we were watchful, we didn't clutch our handbags as if we were expecting to be mugged any minute.

We reserved the right to complain about the weather, and to exchange glances when a drunk sang loudly off-key in the subway. The tourists were largely invisible to us because they swam around inside their own fish tank, "doing" Times Square, the Empire State Building, and the Statue of Liberty.

I hardly warranted the keys to the city, but my status was assured the day a middle-aged woman wearing the trademark backpack and walking shoes approached.

"Excuse me," she asked. "Can you tell me if this is the way to Grand Central?"

I could hardly contain my euphoria. Something about me screamed that I was at home in this great city. She'd mistaken me for a local. Her accent sounded Canadian.

"I certainly can," I said in the tones of a New Yorker being politely helpful to a less fortunate human. "Just keep going straight on down the hill and turn left. You won't miss it."

She was pathetically grateful. I said it was nothing and wished her well for the rest of her vacation.

Having grown up in the country and lived in various cities, I understand the tension between town and country. The gap is intensified when the city happens to be the Big Apple. It's no secret New Yorkers feel superior. I wish I could tell them that from a farmer's perspective, city people are folks who couldn't make it in the country.

The tourists were semi-invisible, but I soon realized New Yorkers acknowledge each other, and I was grateful to be included in a casual way. The Indian family who sold flowers from the market waved as I strode down the hill to buy kitty litter. At the pet supply shop, Doris and I could whittle away half an afternoon discussing the merits of hessian versus carpet scratching posts while Bluebell flicked her tail in the window.

Though the handbag salesmen never invited conversation, I was on nodding terms with some of the beggars, especially the one who sat resting his stump on the steps outside our building most afternoons. Remembering what Greg had told me, I cast an eye over the guy's pockets. If he was carrying a gun, it was a very small one.

Even the people in our building began saying hello. Most of them were single professionals in their mid-thirties. They were far friendlier than most of the neighbors locked in warfare over parking spaces on our dead-end street back in Melbourne. I hadn't seen or heard any more of Patrick downstairs. He was probably out having lunches with Donna Tartt.

For the first time in my life, I became obsessed with laundry—in a good way. It started when I took my coat to the cleaners on East 44th Street to ask if they could remove the paint speckles. They said it would be no problem. When I found out these cheerful chaps washed and dried clothes for $8 a pound, I was down there every few days with another bundle of laundry. Pressed and sealed inside plastic sheeting, my clothes started to look like they belonged to someone else. No longer the Lady of the Food Stains, I had an impressive collection of wire coat hangers, which I recycled back to them.

Living in a city where every minor annoyance was attended to and solved at an affordable price was becoming addictive. One afternoon, I visited the acupuncturist to see if he could sort out my knee. He started by rattling off the names of all the famous people he'd punctured, which reminded me of Patrick. I wondered if name dropping was a New York disease. After taking my pulse, he shook his head and said I had too much male energy and a terrible liver—neither of which sounded like a compliment.

I limped back up the hill afterward, consoling myself with the thought that for any woman in today's world, an overdose of male energy is probably a good thing. I'm quietly shocked feminism didn't take off the way it was supposed to back when we were burning our bras. If today's young women think sending belfies (photos of their bums) to their boyfriends is liberation, I despair for them and their daughters.

As I opened the door to the apartment, I was astonished when a tiny black figure pranced toward me and greeted me with a welcome meow. I cried out and bent to stroke him, but he danced backward across the floor.

Bono jumped on the bed and watched as I flicked the laptop on. The first *Huffington Post* blog was up. Not only that, a swarm of readers had posted comments.

Hi Helen, Bono is ADORABLE! Thanks for writing about rescue cats. So many people think they have to buy animals from pet stores. Though I know you can't bring Bono to Colorado, you're both in my thoughts.

Dear Mrs. Brown, I live in Moscow, Russia, and I have cared for unwanted cats for the past 17 years. They are my best friends. I hope Bono finds the home he deserves.

Hi, I want a cat like Bono, but we have five already and Mom says that's enough. When I grow up I'm going to work in a shelter like Bideawee. Love, Nick, Little Rock, Arkansas, USA, The World, The Universe.

Dear Helen, Our entire vet clinic is in love with Bono! We'd love it if you could take time out to speak at a fundraiser to raise awareness around rescue animals. Arianna, LA.

Hi Helen, Rescue animals are the best. I've had shelter cats all my life. They're so grateful and loving. Sometimes it's been hard to know who's been rescuing who! Buckets of love to you and Bono, Gina, Phoenix, Arizona.

Dear Mrs Brown, I love Bono, but I can't adopt him because I live in Auckland, New Zealand. Instead, I will be visiting our local shelter this weekend. If I can find a cat who looks anything like him, or even one that doesn't, he'll be coming home with me. Keep up the good work. Yours, Andrea.

## Chapter Twenty-four

# EMOTIONAL ACCOUNTANCY

*To love a cat is
to love life itself.*

"Looks like you've got a fan club, Bono," I said.

The cat blinked up at me from his favorite black and white polka dot pillow and mewed. He had always pretended to be deaf when I used his name.

"So, you know your name, after all?" I said closing the laptop. "Hungry?"

My roommate bounced after me as I walked to the fridge. He moved with such grace, he seemed to be surfing on a cloud.

"Have you ever considered a career in modeling?" I asked. "You could have your very own catwalk."

Bono padded across the floorboards and flipped his back leg up in the trademark arabesque. It was good to live with a feline who appreciated my sense of humor.

He lowered his haunches in front of the fridge door and fixed the handle with an expectant gaze.

"What does Monsieur feel like today? A little fish? A slice of chicken, perhaps?"

Bono gave me a sharp meow. As I spooned the chicken into his bowl, he emitted an appreciative purr.

"Such a well-mannered cat," I said, running

my hand over his back. I was gratified to feel the beginnings of a layer of fat under the wiry fur. My famine victim was filling out.

After a quick stop off at the litter box, Bono trotted toward me and pounced on my shoelace. I pulled out Lydia's fishing rod and we wasted a good ten minutes behaving like fools.

He had a lot of energy for a sick cat, but after a while he retreated to his pillow, purring to himself all the way. It was sweet and musical, the sound Mozart would have made if he'd been a cat.

I'd noticed Bono's purring was becoming louder and more frequent these days. As he puttered about the studio, the little cat could hardly stop humming to himself. It was as if he couldn't believe his luck to be in a place where he was fussed over and fed. And yes, now I had to admit it, loved.

I hadn't meant to fall in love with Bono, and now I was beginning to understand why I'd fought so hard not to. Since the cancer, I'd shut myself off from the possibility of loving new things. To love is inevitably to lose, and I wasn't sure I could take any more pain. But Bono was teaching me the whole point of being alive is to remain open to the possibility of love. No matter how much physical and emotional hurt a person has endured, the heart must stay open. It's the whole point of being alive. The alternative is bitterness, isolation, a living death.

A city takes on a different hue when there's love in it. Faces on the street seem softer. The spring breeze is more like a kiss than a knife. Sunset over the skyscrapers gleams as pink as a schoolgirl's lunch box.

The problem with love is sooner or later the heart receives an invoice. Bono was such a demonstrative little fellow, returning him to life in a cage was now out of the question. Which left me two options: (1) Find him adoptive parents through the blog or (2) Failing that, arrange for him to be shipped to Australia in the hope he and Jonah wouldn't scratch each other's eyes out.

The more I investigated option two, the less likely it seemed. Exporting a healthy cat is complicated enough. Even if Bono passed the vet's check, subjecting him to quarantine and harrowing flights could be more than his delicate system could endure. For the moment, I couldn't even think about going back to my old life anyway.

There was an option three. But I needed to talk that one over with Philip. Wild and potentially dangerous, option three involved me staying on in New York, adopting Bono, and hoping my husband and Jonah would follow. Option three would need to be presented to Philip with a great deal of tact and strategic thinking—two things I'm hardly famous for.

Anyway, I didn't need to worry about options

two and three because a woman called Angie had fallen in love with him through the *Huffington Post* blog. I phoned Vida with the exciting news.

"Angie wants to adopt him!"

"That's wonderful!" Vida squealed. "I'm so happy. What part of New York does she live in?"

I scrolled down through Angie's email.

"Berlin. Germany. Do you think that's a problem?"

"Not if she really wants him," Vida said. "I've had friends take cats all over the world. I'll look into it for you."

"Hang on. She's written a postscript. *Though I would love to adopt Bono immediately, I'm afraid my husband is allergic to cats.*"

"Oh," Vida said. "Maybe Bono will have to keep looking."

After a while, the charm of the thirty or so people with feline allergic partners started to wear thin. Why did they bother contacting me if adoption was out of the question? A Florida man wanted to fly up to meet Bono. I wasn't upset when his enthusiasm waned. He resembled one of those silver-haired Facebook suitors who posts self-portraits proclaiming he's "single and looking for fun."

It was as I'd always suspected. To "Like" a cat photo and ooze adjectives online is easy. To show up and take a breathing, vulnerable life in your hands, however, that's a kitten of a different color.

After the second blog post went up and a new tide of Bono worshippers washed in from all over the world, I pinned hopes on Lucy from Brooklyn. She seemed a sensible young woman with a genuine love of animals. She adored Bono's looks, especially his haircut. More important, she wasn't daunted by his prognosis.

On the afternoon she planned to visit, I hurried out to the flower shop and bought acres of red and yellow tulips. As I carried them past Patrick's door, it burst open.

"She's *dead!*" he shouted jubilantly.

I froze and almost dropped the flowers. Though I was aware Patrick was probably borderline eccentric, I hadn't put him in the murderer category. Remembering my journalistic days, I drew a breath, adopted a calm tone, and asked the name of the deceased.

"Maggie Thatcher!" he said, his eyes swiveling wildly behind his glasses.

"You mean the woman who used to be the British prime minister?" I asked, immensely relieved he wouldn't be asking to borrow towels and help him hoist an oversized trash bag down the garbage chute.

"Good riddance, I say. We *hated* her in Ireland," he said, beckoning me into his lair. "This calls for a whiskey."

Though I didn't love Margaret Thatcher when she was in power, I wasn't eager to dance on her grave—or anyone else's for that matter. Besides, hard as I've tried, I've never managed to appreciate the subtleties of whiskey.

Patrick must have sensed I was finding his vehemence perturbing.

"Been poaching in Central Park, have we now?" he asked, softening his tone and casting his gaze over my tulips.

I told him the wake would have to wait for another day on account of my visitor. I regretted saying the word the moment it left my lips.

"And what sort of a visitor would that be?" he asked, folding his arms and leaning against his doorframe as if he had all afternoon, which he undoubtedly did.

A friend of a friend, I said. Not in the publishing world, so nobody he'd know.

Patrick made a point of reminding me I owed him a book, and perhaps I could bring it down for afternoon tea tomorrow around three. I nodded and hurried upstairs to prepare the apartment for our important guest.

Bono greeted me at the door and bounced toward me with his tail aloft.

"This is the beginning of your new life," I said, sinking the tulips into vases.

Before long, the place resembled a house and garden show. Sensing something was up, Bono even let me brush the end of his tail.

The cat stretched out like a movie star on the

window ledge while I played Scrabble on my iPad and drank too much coffee. The light softened to shades of lilac as the outlines of office workers in the other building packed up their desks and left for the day.

An hour later, I sent Lucy a text, but there was no reply. As hope faded to disappointment, I wasn't angry with her. She hadn't meant to let us down. This experience was probably just a piece of flint she'd tripped over on her road to maturity. Perhaps now she understood the gulf between meaning well and doing something can be as deep as the Grand Canyon.

## Chapter Twenty-five

# GOLDEN TOWERS

*A cat is no stranger
to jealousy.*

Bono had become king of our studio. His tummy had rounded out, and his fur seemed glossier—not that he'd let me brush it thoroughly, let alone trim his nails. Though he still refused to let me pick him up, I'd never seen such a happy, grateful feline.

Every night he slept on the pillow next to mine. I woke each morning to the touch of a paw gently patting my eyelids, as if Bono was checking to confirm I was still breathing. He'd then sit back on his pillow and watch with appalled interest as his giantess housemate yawned and groaned herself awake.

When the laptop bleeped with an incoming Skype call, I scrunched my hair and hoped Philip wouldn't die of fright at the sight of my early morning dishevelment. He'd been working late and was looking impeccably handsome in his suit.

"Great tie," I said. "Where did it come from?"

Bono emitted a happy meow from beside my feet.

"You bought it for me, remember?"

Philip's computer wobbled and a large, angry-looking Jonah face glowered at me.

"What's the matter, boy?" I asked.

"He heard the other cat," Philip said, stroking Jonah and trying to ease him into a sitting position on his lap.

"Oh, Jonah!" I said. "You don't need to worry about Bono. You're such a beautiful boy!"

Jonah's ears pricked up. He'd always been a sucker for flattery.

"And look at those eyes," I added, trying to ignore Bono, who was now winding himself around my ankles. "How did they get so blue?"

When Bono meowed a second time, Jonah pressed his face into the screen and growled like a bear.

"Don't be silly, Jonah," I said. "Bono's your friend."

As Jonah's eyes narrowed to a pair of turquoise slits, I could feel option two going down the drain. No way would Jonah welcome a rival cat into his life.

"Have you found him a home yet?" Philip asked.

"I thought I had. A girl said she wanted him," I said. "But she didn't show up."

"That's a shame," Philip said, shaking his head. His disappointment seemed genuine.

"I've got a crazy neighbor," I said, to lift the mood. "His name's Patrick. He's Irish and such a namedropper. Reckons he knows every writer that ever lived in New York."

"He's a writer?"

"I don't think so. He just drinks with writers, and sleeps with them."

"He lives downstairs?" Philip asked in a tone sober enough to serve at a vicarage tea party.

In every relationship, there's a lover and a beloved. With Philip I'd always been the lover—adoring, insecure, and terrified he'd be swept away by a woman who understood the rules of rugby and had gym-honed thighs. Women friends were constantly telling me how lucky I was to be married to him, and I had to agree. He's a fantastic husband and father whose kindheartedness and patience stretch to infinity.

Since the cancer, however, I'd released a lot of that anxiety. Life's too short to fret over stuff that might never happen.

Cancer had taught me the only thing worse than dying is forgetting to live every day to the fullest. Paradoxically, because of the illness, I felt more alive than ever. The prospect of being a woman alone, abandoned, or otherwise, was no longer terrifying. Not only was I surviving New York, I was relishing the solitude. I didn't have to make excuses or explain myself to anyone. Nobody expected me carry aspirin in my pocket in case they got a headache. And with Bono for a housemate, I was hardly lonely.

For the first time, it dawned on me that Philip

might have an insecurity or two of his own. Whenever I'd joked he might trade me in for a cover model on an outdoor hiking magazine, he'd retaliate with the suggestion I'd run off with someone . . . literary.

"Oh no!" I said. "It's not like that. He's probably gay."

In truth, Patrick was a flirt and almost certainly straight.

"In fact, I'm sure he's gay," I added. "He's interested in my clothes."

Jonah yowled again. Philip put his head to one side.

"Not in *that* way!" I said. "You know how gay men like shopping."

"You go shopping with him?"

Jonah emitted an uncharacteristic hiss, which had no effect on Bono who was lying on his back toying with a piece of scrap paper.

"*NO!* I'm having a cup of tea down at his place later to celebrate Margaret Thatcher's death. That's all."

"I didn't know you care about Margaret Thatcher?"

"I don't! I didn't . . . it's a New York thing," I lied. "They're all doing it here at the moment. Except most of them are drinking whiskey."

There was an awkward silence.

He loosened his tie and talked about getting dinner. In fact, he looked tired.

As we signed off with reciprocal I-love-yous, Jonah shot me a death look.

That afternoon, I went downstairs and tapped on the DO NOT SLAM DOORS! sign. If only Philip could meet Patrick he'd know he had nothing to worry about. I waited a minute or two, but there was no reply. Relieved, I placed a copy of my book on the floor under the sign and tiptoed away.

I had plenty to do tidying myself up for the pet store book launch. Book signings make me nervous at the best of times. Once, in small town New Zealand, a woman who'd waited twenty minutes in line bent over and whispered in my ear that one day she'd be the author sitting in the chair, and I'd be the one paying homage to her. I told her I'd happily swap places.

One of the things I worry about is that readers will be disappointed when they meet me in the flesh. I'm hardly going to post my ugliest photos on social media. Besides, I'm not always funny or profound, and I can be a bit deaf these days. Then there is the matter of how much time to spend with each individual. If they have traveled on horseback through a war zone to meet me, they deserve more than a brisk smile and a signature scribbled inside the book they have just bought. I worry about spelling names wrong. Or, in the panic of it all, momentarily forgetting the name of a friend who has come along to give support. I've tried dealing with it by asking who she'd like me to sign the copy for. It doesn't help when she puts her arm around my shoulder and says, "Just me."

Quite often, people want to share their stories of grief, and these encounters are incredibly precious. We exchange hugs and sometimes weep together. In many cases, all they seem to need is reassurance they are not alone. In this world that worships success, death is regarded as the ultimate failure. I can never give these souls enough time. Together we are learning that without pain and loss, life would be a carnival ride with no meaning.

On the other hand, a reader might want to regale me with details of an argument he's having with a neighbor over barking dogs. If the reader happens to be Polish, Japanese, or German and a translator's involved, the exchange becomes even more bewildering. That's when the publisher's representative, if she's on the ball, will step in and steer him toward the drinks table.

Probably the worst thing that can happen at a book signing is nobody shows up. Still, that was unlikely to happen in New York because of the pet shop setting. At worst, a few goldfish would be in attendance.

At least I was pleased with my new outfit. The electric blue jacket was long enough to cover my backside, and I couldn't go wrong with black trousers. The only thing that remained to sort out was my hair. Before leaving Australia, I'd promised my Melbourne hairdresser, Brendan, I'd try out a salon whose website he was obsessed with.

I arrived early (as usual) so I crossed Fifth Avenue between 56th and 57th Streets and entered the golden bowels of Trump Tower. With its cliffs of gleaming glass, the foyer was the modern equivalent of a pharaoh's tomb. Strains of a plaintive Elvis wafted through invisible loudspeakers. Intrigued, I rode the escalator to a Starbucks on the mezzanine floor and ordered a cappuccino.

Though I was familiar with the wigged tycoon who fired people on TV, it was clear nobody was ever going to take the man seriously. Not when he owned a fifty-eight-story building with a top floor marked sixty-eight. It was like a teenage boy swearing six inches was really eight.

Over at the hairdresser's, Marcello the mustachioed colorist draped a black wrap over my shoulders.

"You must have had very light hair when you were a child," he said, running a comb through my roots.

"How can you tell?" I asked.

"It's just a thing I have," he said.

"Like . . . an invisible power?"

"You could call it that," he said. "I can tell people's nationality from their hair, too."

"Really? Did you learn that in a course?"

Back home, Brendan was always going on courses.

"Hell no," said Marcello, flashing his Mediterranean eyes at the mirror. "It's something I do. I'm never wrong."

"Wow! That's amazing," I said. "Can you tell where I'm from?"

"Of course," he said, sounding like a magician about to cast a spell.

I waited breathless as Marcello inspected my scalp. I could hardly wait for him to settle the debate that had kept our family arguing for generations: Were we Scottish or French?

"German," Marcello announced.

"What?" I said, astonished. "Are you sure?"

"Without a doubt," he said, raising his comb and pointing it at me like a wand. "You're German."

A delicately built Canadian girl was in charge of drying my hair.

"Do you have a cat?" she shouted over the buzz of the machine.

I nearly jumped out of the chair. Everyone in the salon seemed to be psychic.

"How on Earth did you know?" I asked.

She laughed and pointed at the strands of Bono's hair on my sleeve. Though she'd moved from Toronto to make it in the Big Apple, her new life was nowhere near as glamorous as she'd hoped. With the commuting and long hours, she was pushing to survive on less and less sleep. No wonder New Yorkers went neurotic or turned to pills, she said.

I'd never had a book signing in a pet shop before. Thanks to the publishing team's understanding, Bono was roosting on his pillow back in our apartment. A pair of handsome black understudies and a tortoiseshell had stepped in on his behalf and taken center stage in the store. Like Bono, they were up for rehoming. Though shoppers circled their cage with interest, nobody was willing to walk out the door with a new pet in tow. It was a sobering reminder how naive I'd been to even try to find a full-time mom for a cat with compromised kidneys.

My books were on display toward the back of the store. I sat at the table there and lifted my pen.

"Where's Bono?" the voice had a sharpness that put me on guard.

"He couldn't come here today," I said, glancing up to see an older woman in a gray raincoat.

"I've been reading about him in *Huffington Post*. I've seen the photos," she said.

"Are you interested in adopting him?" I asked.

"No, but what's the point of having this event without him being here?" her tone was taking on a threatening edge.

"I'm sure you understand he's not in great health," I said.

"Not good enough!" she shouted.

I glanced sideways for a potential rescuer, but Michaela was engaged in conversation with a man who wanted to know if the black cats could be separated, or if they had to be adopted together.

"Go and get Bono *right now!*" the woman shouted.

"I'm sorry, but . . ."

To my relief, Karen ferried me to the safety of a storeroom, while Vida took the woman aside and talked her down.

Bono was stepping into more lives and in different ways than I'd imagined possible.

## Chapter Twenty-six

# THE FEAR MACHINE

*A cat knows when
hugs are needed.*

No wonder primitive people imagined they were living on the back of a giant, unpredictable monster. Most of the time, the dragon sleeps, allowing us to drift along in a state of semiconsciousness. Absorbed in multitudes of diversions, we forget about the monster. But every now and then, sometimes after years of sleep, the monster flicks its tail and tosses everyday reality into the air. It leaves a trail of panic and destruction. Those who survive are forever changed.

April 15, 2013, began like any other Monday. I flung the curtains open to examine a watery looking sky that promised sunshine later on. After filling Bono's bowls, I sifted through his latest raft of online fan mail. Admirers from Germany, France, Italy, Australia, New Zealand, and various corners of the United States gushed superlatives, but none were interested in becoming prospective parents. My month in the apartment was halfway through. Finding another place that would take a cat would be next to impossible. I worried we were running out of time. Bono leapt onto the table beside me to clean his teeth on the edge of my laptop screen.

I once decided a home can be any size providing I could walk around naked in it. With that luxury out of my price range in New York, I huddled in the shadows near the kitchenette. The attempt at modesty was futile, anyway. Though the anonymous workers in the opposite building intrigued me, they'd shown no interest in the world outside their windows. Besides, I thought it unlikely anyone would want to watch a sturdy midlife woman struggle into her pants.

After breakfast at the deli, I wandered down to the post office near Grand Central to send off another crop of *Frozen* cards to Annie and Stella. Even if they didn't read them, I wanted the next generation to understand there was such a thing as paper and stamps. The response so far had been mild. I wondered if their parents were fed up with my postcards clogging their mailbox.

Later in the afternoon, on my way back to the apartment, I noticed a change to the city's mood. People on the street seemed on edge and unusually subdued. I bought a falafel from the shop near the corner, slid the key in the heart-shaped lock, and hurried upstairs to Bono.

As I sat on the sofa bed, a shaken Obama appeared on the TV screen. He exhorted people to stay calm and assured viewers the perpetrators would be found.

Bono sprang on my lap and nibbled at my falafel, so far untouched and tepid inside its foil wrapper. I watched in disbelief as images unfolded on a grueling loop. Crowds cheered as runners crossed a finish line. A violent explosion. Screams. In an instant, jubilation became shock as a plume of black smoke rose behind the athletes. A few seconds later, there was a second deadly explosion.

Ever since 1879, the Boston Marathon has been held on Patriot's Day, the third Monday in April. As the world's oldest annual marathon, it attracts around half a million spectators. The 30,000 participants create a memorable spectacle, but the 2013 marathon would be etched in history for all the wrong reasons.

My heart ached for the families of the three spectators who'd been killed. Their shock would be immeasurable. Combined with the devastating suffering sudden grief brings, they'd also have to confront their own justifiable outrage. More than 200 others were injured that day. Sixteen people lost their limbs, the youngest being a seven-year-old girl.

Tragedy can bring out extraordinary compassion in some. As the images played over again, I noticed after the explosions, some people were actually running toward the devastation rather than away from it. Without thinking twice, these heroes were risking their lives to help others.

Philip's anxious face appeared on my laptop screen.

"Are you okay?"

"We're fine. They made the bombs out of pressure cookers," I said.

"Like the one we used to steam corned beef in?" he asked.

"Yes, they packed them with shrapnel and nails," I said. "Then they stashed them into backpacks and left them on the scene."

Philip shook his head.

"It's the first time anyone has used that type of homemade device on US soil," I said.

"Do they know who did it?"

"Not yet. They could be hiding anywhere. The cops seem to think they're heading to New York."

I noticed a flash of concern in his eyes.

"Guess it's the best place to go if they want to hide in a crowd," I said.

"Do you want to see if I can get you a flight home?" he asked.

"Don't worry," I said. "We'll be fine."

Afterward as I climbed into bed, my thoughts turned to the broken window lock I'd forgotten to complain about. The days had been too full and stimulating for me to bother contacting the rental agency.

Bono nuzzled my neck and purred.

"You're not alone," he seemed to be saying. "I'm with you. Neither of us is on this planet for much longer. Let's not waste time being scared."

For the first time, Bono let me hug him. His

warmth ran up my arms. I could feel the little heart pattering under his shaven ribs. On some level, Bono understood I needed comforting the way another miniature black cat, Cleo, had decades earlier in the harsh days after Sam's death.

I'd since heard stories from readers of how, through life's most challenging times, animals have tuned into their sorrow and done everything in their power to help. When my brother Jim was given a grim cancer diagnosis, his English sheepdog Tash sensed what was going on. Month after month, Tash lay at his side. They died within days of each other and are buried together in a country cemetery near our hometown. As graves go, it's a good one, being right next door to a pub and having an excellent view of a mountain we grew up under.

Even if a villain slid the window open during the night and murdered me, it would be nothing compared to the untold suffering going on in other parts of the world, including Boston. There was peace and freedom in accepting my insignificance. In the larger canvas of life, I was a mere paint speck. Bono sprang off the bed and trotted off to the Bunker.

Next to a crossword, I find a game of Scrabble the best sedative. I reached for the iPad. The word "terrorist" has minimal value. Each of the nine letters is worth only one point, compared to (for example) "hero," which if the *h* is set on a triple letter score, can be worth fifteen points.

The first time I heard the *t* word was probably back in the 1970s when the IRA was planting bombs in London railway stations. I've never liked the look of the word, or its melodramatic overuse. Mass murderers don't deserve a noun that implies they have a higher mission. They're thugs whose attention-seeking antics are rewarded by the ratings-hungry media who are eager to feed off a gullible public's fears.

For terrorism to lose its edge, people need to toughen up and be realistic. According to the Global Terrorism Index, there were 18,000 deaths worldwide from so-called acts of terror in the year of the Boston bombings (most being in Iraq). In the same year, the World Health Organization reported 1.3 million deaths from road traffic. Almost every case involves the tragic loss of innocents and leaves a trail of broken-hearted families. I'm not suggesting road traffic should be banned, but in a logical world if we were going to be terrified by anything it would be cars.

If some wild-eyed kid who called himself a terrorist was about to climb the fire escape that night, I'd have a thing or two to say to him.

I arranged the bedside table half tidily, in case a homicide squad might need to inspect the place in a few hours. Once the light was out, Bono jumped back on the bed and nestled into the pillow next to mine. I drifted off to the regular squeak of his snoring. We slept soundly—apart from my regulation visit to the bathroom.

Next morning, I was lured onto the street to witness the mood of a nervous nation in mourning. In cafés and shops, the tension was palpable. Whenever a siren could be heard, there was a ripple of alarm, an exchange of looks.

Images of planes smashing into buildings were still sharp in many minds. Mostly people were keeping their heads down, but every few seconds a construction worker or a woman in a suit would glance up at the sky.

On the corner of Second Avenue, as I stood waiting for the lights to change, a nervous woman with a nose ring pointed at something above our heads.

"What's that?" she asked.

I glanced up at what appeared to be an extra wire draped between the utility poles. It didn't seem connected to any electrical services. I had no idea what it was, but sometimes a senior person's role is simply to reassure.

"Could be one of those eruv wires," I said.

"A what?" she asked.

"You know how orthodox Jews aren't supposed to do anything on the Sabbath, not even cook or push a stroller."

The woman stared blankly at me.

"I think if they stay inside the boundary of an eruv wire on the Sabbath they're allowed to do all that stuff," I said.

She didn't seem comforted by my theory.

Panic has its uses. Our ancestors needed to be scared of wild animals in order to survive. In the twenty-first century anxiety is superfluous most of the time, except perhaps when we're diving into a wall of traffic. That doesn't deny the fact we're programmed to experience it—though not always to our own benefit. Whenever I felt unnerved by the city's edginess, I turned to Bono and did my best to follow his example. He wasn't worried.

Fear consumes too much energy. It's a manipulative tool used by politicians, advertisers, so-called terrorists, and anyone else wanting control over others. When people are frightened they become powerless cringers with no dignity. Once on a bus, I saw a man who had to change seats because he was terrified of a butterfly.

It's disheartening to overhear full-grown adults use "scary" to describe everything from phone bills to cigarette smoke. The emotion filters down to become fear of eating the wrong food, not working hard enough, or being too fat, not rich, or smart enough. Compulsive fear erodes into stress. While I sympathize to a point, it's time people started living like cats. A homeless feline with a lion haircut and a lousy prognosis was to me a perfect example of how to make the most of being alive.

Days of paranoia crawled by. Black limos slid around the corner to the UN Building, which had been barricaded like a medieval castle. Did they know something? Down at Grand Central rows of helmeted men wore black bulletproof gear and carried assault rifles. It was like living in a *Star Wars* movie.

People were warned to report suspicious packages, but at night the streets were lined with the same old piles of garbage bags, each one large enough to harbor several bombs. They were so much part of the nocturnal landscape New Yorkers hardly noticed them.

There was collective relief after the first shoot-out when Tamerlan Tsarnaev, age 26, was run over and killed by his younger brother, Dzhokhar, in a stolen car. Anxiety returned to gnaw at the nation's soul with the announcement that Dzhokhar, age 19, was still on the run. When he was discovered hiding inside a boat in a suburban backyard, the saga ground to a conclusion. It had been a long four days—and would have been longer if the murderous brothers had achieved their goal of traveling to New York to bomb Times Square.

# Chapter Twenty-seven

# HOLDING AND BREATHING

*A cat has many lives to choose from.*

I sometimes wonder how I would have handled the aftermath of the Boston bombings without Bono's warm and trusting companionship. When things are in turmoil, sometimes all you have to do is stay still, hold someone you love . . . and breathe.

Basking in the sun on his pillow, my feline friend reminded me to savor the moment. As I watched him skip about the apartment, he taught me the most powerful way to experience life is from a place of gratitude. He'd released the wounds of the past and was simply happy to be away from the stresses of living in a shelter.

As for his future, I was doing enough worrying for the both of us.

Returning Bono to Bideawee to spend the rest of his life in a cage would feel like the ultimate failure. In a way, we were both prisoners on the run. I'd come to New York to escape a cage of my own making. With just ten days before the lease expired on our pet-friendly apartment, time was running out for both of us.

I pictured myself bringing his carrier back along the river to Bideawee, and burst into tears. But this is America, I thought, dabbing my eyes with a towel. Bono's story had to have a happy ending.

When I called Michaela, the warmth in her voice made me want to cry again.

"The blog's not working," I said.

"What do you mean?" she asked. "Vida tells me more than 22 million people are reading your posts."

The number was mind-boggling.

"That can't be right," I said. "Surely she counted the zeros wrong?"

"According to Vida, the number's on the conservative side," Michaela said.

I tried to imagine the entire population of Australia squeezed into our tiny studio. One thing was certain. There wouldn't be enough cups to go round. If the figure was right, and Michaela assured me there was no reason to doubt it, everything I'd ever felt about the Internet was confirmed. Millions of voyeuristic eyeballs could roll but hearts remained untouched.

"It's done nothing for Bono other than make him famous," I said. "He's no closer to finding a home than he ever was."

There was silence at the other end of the line. My friend was probably editing a worthy manuscript that was about to change the world.

"Don't worry," she said.

I had to admire Michaela. Compared to her, Pollyanna was a pessimist.

"I have a friend who's interested in meeting

him," she added. "I forwarded Bono's photo to her. She can't stop oohing and ahhing."

Her words had the impact of a feather landing on an elephant's hide. The whole world was infatuated with Bono. He needed love with its sleeves rolled up.

The days lurched into fast-forward as the city settled back into its old rhythms. I became like a mouse in a wheel scurrying from museum to theater to landmark while I tried to make up my mind. Once the lease had run out on the apartment, I'd have to return Bono to the shelter and fly back to Australia.

Unless, I went for option three and rented somewhere to stay until I found another pet-friendly apartment. Maybe Michaela would agree to have Bono for a week or two, or he could move back temporarily to Bideawee until I found us a home.

Large museums overwhelm me, and libraries can be intimidating, but the Morgan Library & Museum on Madison Avenue at 36th Street is the perfect size. A pleasant stroll from our apartment, it had become one of my favorite haunts.

As I wandered through its exquisite rooms graced with original manuscripts by Mark Twain, Tolkien, and Beethoven, I would lose all sense of time. The Morgan is the cultural universe in miniature.

Like so much else of value in New York, the

library stems back to a wealthy individual. Pierpont Morgan was a financier fixated on collecting early manuscripts and old master drawings. After his death in 1913, his glorious collection, along with its purpose-built palazzo, was donated to the public. The museum has continued to collect and expand without losing its intimacy—and the excellent café was never crowded.

After a dose of Morgan bliss one day, I ended up in a wonderful shoe shop where the smiling assistant didn't blink when I confessed to size eleven feet. He spread an array of summer mules in dazzling colors at my feet. All were my size. I felt like Dorothy in the Emerald City. I bought a silver pair that was so comfortable, I had to go back for a second pair in cobalt blue.

"What do you think?" I asked, swiveling the laptop so Philip could see my new blue shoes.

"They look stunning," he said, but I could tell he was being polite. Men never understand the thrill of new shoes.

"How are Annie and Stella liking their *Frozen* cards?" I asked.

"I haven't heard," he said. "But Lydia can't stop talking about Bono and the wonderful time she had over there."

We lapsed into silence. Overcome with a compulsion to fill it, I blurted out option three.

"I can't leave Bono."

Silence.

"What do you mean?" he asked.

"I'm not leaving here until I find him a home."

The words sounded more powerful than they had when they'd been inside my head. But I wasn't about to take them back. Philip straightened his shoulders.

"I see," he said after another long pause. "And what's going to happen if you can't find him one?"

I grabbed a tissue from the bedside table and blew my nose. There was no way to wrap option three in pretty paper with a ribbon on it.

"I'll just have to stay here," I said.

"How's your neighbor?" he asked, changing the subject.

"Who?"

"The Irish writer."

"What?! He's not a writer. He's just a—"

"Oh, I'm sorry. There's another call on the line," Philip said. "We're making an important acquisition."

I knew better than to compete with that priority. We blew air kisses and said good-bye. There was no chance for me to tell him I hadn't seen my neighbor lately. The copy of my book had disappeared from Patrick's doorstep, so he'd obviously read the thing and hated it. I hadn't had a whiff of him since the demise of Maggie Thatcher. Surely Philip realized option three had nothing to do with Patrick.

*Chapter Twenty-eight*

# CALL OF THE WILD

*A cat sometimes
needs a savior.*

I was nervous about sharing my plans with Michaela. She'd think I'd gone bonkers. But I needed to tell her how much Bono meant to me now, and that he was the reason I was going to stay in New York. When she invited me to meet her at the Central Park Zoo, I thought it would be the perfect setting to tell her my news.

The zoo started back in the 1860s when it was a depository for creatures too unpredictable to squeeze inside a parlor, such as a bear and some swans. Before long, celebrities decided to enhance their reputations by adding to the collection. General Custer donated a rattlesnake.

As the cab pulled up outside the zoo, the first thing I saw was Michaela's red jacket glowing like a beacon. She greeted me warmly and we bustled through the gates like a pair of excited schoolgirls. Central Park Zoo was smaller than I'd expected. At six-and-a-half acres, there's something quaint and endearing about the place. Even though it was upgraded with naturalistic exhibits in the 1980s, it retains the aura of a Victorian menagerie.

After pausing to admire the sea lions cavorting in their pool, we bounced through an indoor rain forest. Michaela's plan was clear, however. Cat woman to the core, she wanted to show me the snow leopards.

"There he is!" Michaela whispered, pointing out a magnificent snow leopard crouched on a rocky outcrop. "Isn't he beautiful?"

If God exists, She must have been on a creative high when She invented the combination of black and white fur and sapphire eyes. The disdain in his steady blue gaze reminded me of Jonah in one of his snooty moods.

"Has there been any more interest in Bono?" Michaela asked.

"Plenty," I replied. "But no takers."

"I was hoping you'd say that," she said, raising her phone to take a snapshot of the leopard. He straightened his spine like a fashion model and arranged his head at an elegant angle for her.

"It's a disaster," I said, confident my hearing had failed me again. "He's such a great little guy, but I think I've found a way around it. I've decided to—"

"Remember I told you about my friend Monique?" Michaela interrupted. "You'd love her. She's an extraordinary person. She lives in my building and takes care of my cats when Gene and I are away. She loves black cats."

"Really?" I have a soft spot for people who like black cats.

"Her precious kitty Onyx passed away a few years ago and she still keeps his dishes and litter boxes where they always were."

The snow leopard leapt off his rock and disappeared into the foliage. "She adores the photos you posted of Bono. And I've told her what a lovely cat he is."

I thought of Michaela lying on her stomach peering under the bed. It made me worry she might have oversold Bono's charm.

"She's interested in adopting him."

"Really? Does she know how sick he is?"

"Monique's a nurse. She specializes in infectious diseases and her husband Berry's an internist and pediatrician. A little kidney failure's nothing to them."

"They must be amazing," I said.

"They are, and I'd love to have Bono for a neighbor. That way I could keep him in my life."

It sounded wonderful, but when things seem too good to be true, they usually are.

"I can't promise anything," Michaela added.

Peering into the bushes for another glimpse of the snow leopard, I could feel option three starting to wobble on its foundations. I'd always thought I'd be overjoyed if Bono found a loving home. Now it was in the cards, I wasn't so sure. With him adopted, there'd be no reason for me to stay and extend the glorious highs of freedom in New York. I'd be just another face in the human soup pouring down Fifth Avenue.

I was reluctant to welcome serious contenders into the life Bono and I had created in our scruffy apartment. Still, if I'd had to choose anyone to trust his future with, a nurse and a doctor would be near the top of the list.

"You know how shy he is," I said.

"Monique and Bono will have to make their own decisions about each other," Michaela said, laughing.

We wandered toward the three brick arches supporting the famous Delacorte Clock. An updated version of a medieval European clock tower, the timepiece features a collection of whimsical animal sculptures that "dance" to various melodies on the hour.

"She'd like to drop by and meet him sometime," Michaela added. "How about tomorrow morning around 10:30?"

Surely this was a joke. Who was Monique anyway, and why hadn't she been in touch earlier?

I glanced up at a pair of bronze monkeys on top of the tower. They struck the hour on a large bell. We stepped aside to let a small family move in front of us. Two little girls about the same age as our granddaughters chattered at each other in French. The music started and we watched the animals spin past, oblivious to the follies of human concerns. Among them was of all things, a kangaroo, complete with a joey in her pouch, blowing on a horn.

It took a few seconds to recognize the tune: "What the World Needs Now Is Love."

## Chapter Twenty-nine

# LAST CHANCE

*A cat is immune to
the sound of a ticking clock.*

A person who lives in an old house invariably dreams of owning one with windows that do not rattle. Someone who spends days in a townhouse with sleek, functional lines longs for a home with character and a scrabble of roses over a white picket fence.

So why was a happily married woman approaching 60 living out a fantasy about running away from home to New York? Maybe I was chasing after a youth never lived, undergoing some kind of hormonal meltdown, escaping responsibility, or running away from my old buddy, death.

Having grown up under a snow-capped mountain in rural New Zealand, I'd never regarded Australia as my soul home. I considered the Australian landscape too vast and dry, the sky too huge. The lakes and rivers of my beautiful homeland ran through my veins. Besides, few things rile New Zealanders more than Australia claiming one of its own.

But when I saw that bronze kangaroo on the Delacorte Clock, something shifted in me. The five years we'd expected to stay in Australia when we moved there in 1997 had somehow stretched to sixteen. We arrived with a small black cat named Cleo, who watched over our unfolding lives. The five candles I'd placed on Katharine's birthday cake a few months after our arrival had suddenly become ten, and then sixteen. Anxious nights before school exams had morphed into decisions over what university courses to take. Tears and prayers through Rob's ulcerative colitis surgery melted into relief as he gained strength during the months of recovery. There were girlfriends, and then, as our daughters blossomed into womanhood, nervous young men standing on our doorstep. The happiness of Rob's engagement to Chantelle was mingled with sadness at Cleo's departure.

Kids had left home, but our house had become more a rock pool than an empty nest. The tide washed in to fill vacant bedrooms with granddaughters having sleepovers, family from New Zealand, and visitors from various parts of the world. Through all the seasons, there had hardly been time for Philip and I to notice each other. When things were tough, we'd simply clung to each other. Through other phases, when we were lulled into robotic routine, we'd forgotten to hold each other close, and a cool breeze would waft between us. We'd changed, too, of course. He'd lost most of his hair, I'd shed a breast, but superficial deficits were nothing compared to the things we'd gained. Through the decades we'd learned to forgive our differences, accept them, and in some cases even cherish them.

Once, the sight of a bronze kangaroo would have had no more effect on me than the hippopotamus and penguin circling the clock with it. But after fifteen years, I realized it was no longer a case of choosing between being a New Zealander or an Australian, but a matter of belonging to both countries.

We'd traveled back to New Zealand as often as we could to spend precious time with friends and family, but most of the important and banal things in life had happened to us while we were living in Australia.

Perhaps the greatest miracle was that in this age of mobility all three of our offspring, including their partners and our grandchildren, lived in the same city we did. New York was beguiling, but the prospect of passing months without the joy of meeting Katharine for an impromptu coffee, sitting in on Lydia's Tuesday meditation class, or answering a casual phone call from Rob on his way home from work. That was altogether a different litter of kittens.

Either way, I wasn't about to give up on Bono. And when I was honest with myself, Monique was his best and, realistically, last chance. The following morning, Saturday, I slid into my silver shoes and dashed across the road to the flower shop. The manager always seemed surprised when someone wanted to actually buy his blooms. It was as if he'd put them out for decorative purposes only. His tubs of daffodils beamed golden optimism. They looked luckier than tulips. I took two bunches home and stuffed them in the vase beside the fireplace.

Bono watched bemused while I mopped the floor, and sprinkled lavender oil inside the Bunker.

"You've got to be on your best behavior," I said, straightening the nest of papers beside my laptop. "No hiding, okay?"

Desperate to impress, I went into the bathroom and applied a second layer of powder to my nose. An anxious face peered back at me through the gloomy mirror. I ran a comb through my hair, inserted a pair of confident earrings, and applied a circle of lipstick.

We'd been let down before. Even if Monique showed up, she was probably just curious. What could possibly be in this for her? Jon's words echoed inside my head—only a saint would give Bono a home.

The door buzzed ten minutes early. To my horror, my housemate shot straight under the bed.

## Chapter Thirty

# FROM ANOTHER LIFETIME

*A cat who finds his
soul mate is lucky indeed.*

The first thing I noticed about Monique was her halo. Now, maybe my sight is going, but I'm seeing halos more often. I think it's true some people have them. It's not just a New Age thing. Back in medieval times, artists painted halos around saints as a matter of course.

Halos are more common than you'd think. I see them around babies, old people, and birds. The guy who works in the organic shop has a halo, and so does the road worker who meets my eye with a smile. Sometimes, I've wondered if animals look for halos, too, and if that, along with body language, is how they decide whether to trust a human.

I've yet to see a halo around a person on a mobile phone. There's nothing like the deadening ping of a text message to suck the magic out of a situation.

The first person to introduce me to the power of light was His Holiness the Dalai Lama. Back in May 1992, I assumed my boss would be thrilled I had a chance to score an exclusive interview with him.

When she shrugged and said, "The Dalai Who?" I was crestfallen. To add to the complications, the only possible gap in the great man's timetable was going to be near the end of his tour when he was in Dunedin, near the bottom of the South Island. I was at the other end of the country, near the top of the North Island, in Auckland. On top of that, I was pregnant and a breath away from the seven-month flying ban.

I took annual leave and flew off to Dunedin on a wintry afternoon. After an anxious twenty-four hours holed up in a motel, the call came and I was escorted into his presence.

The room shimmered with radiance that seemed to be emanating from the man who calls himself a simple Buddhist monk. I'd seen versions of that light in maternity wards, around deathbeds, and often around animals. The only name I can give it is pure love. He took my hand and greeted me with a gaze so intense, it was like looking into the eyes of a wild bird. It seemed as if we'd known each other for centuries. No stranger to suffering, the former leader of Tibet fled his country as a young man and lives in exile. Many thousands of his followers have been slaughtered. Yet his deep, mahogany laughter springs from the core of the Earth. I keep a recording of the interview in my desk drawer. Whenever I need consolation, or simply to be reminded what it means to be alive, I click the play button and listen to his laughter.

When I asked him where women fit into his religion, he adjusted his robe and fixed me with those blazing eyes. Everything in the universe since the beginning of time, he said, has sprung from pure light. That light, he assured me, is female.

So, while I'm willing to accept the sun may have been filtering through the stairwell in an unusual way that day, as far as I was concerned, Monique had a halo. What's more, her eyes were shining with excitement. With her dark hair tied back and a broad, open smile, she had something of Michelle Obama about her. Not only did I warm to her on the spot, I felt I'd known this woman through many lifetimes.

"I'm sorry, Bono's a bit shy," I said.

"Where is he?" Monique asked.

"He's not always like this," I replied, pointing at the bed. "He takes a while to get used to people."

Disappointment flashed across her face. She had every reason to turn around and leave. I was grateful when she accepted my offer of a cup of tea. Sitting on the sofa, Monique told me she'd always loved black cats. I said I felt the same way, and tried to explain the impact of Cleo on our lives. Monique's Cleo equivalent had been a treasured feline called Onyx. He'd died five years earlier. The heartbreak of losing him had been shattering. She kept Onyx's ashes in her apartment, and maintained a shrine to him in her kitchen.

Some people have cats. Others have soul mates wrapped in fur. Onyx clearly fell into the second category. Monique hadn't been able to consider opening her heart to another feline.

"But I think I might be ready now," she said.

As I poured hot water over the tea bags, it occurred to me that five years is a long time to grieve over a cat. Monique was no lightweight in her commitment to animals. She was exactly the sort of person Bono needed. He'd be incredibly lucky if she offered him a home—if only he could summon the courage to step out into the open and introduce himself.

"Not very friendly, is he?" Monique said as I poured her a second cup of tea.

Bono's chances were evaporating as fast as the steam over our cups. I felt like grabbing the mop and chasing him out from under there. But all Monique would see then would be an angry and frightened cat. After a while, conversation dwindled. Monique sighed and reached for her handbag. Any hope I'd had sank to my ankles.

"There he is!" Monique whispered.

Bono trotted out from under the other side of the bed as if he was on a shopping errand that had nothing to do with us. He paused beside the fireplace. I held my breath. Though he'd lost interest in it since Lydia had stuffed it with plastic bags, I was anxious he might decide to liven up the afternoon with a second attempt.

He admired the daffodils, and arched his tail in a fetching curve.

"Look at that haircut!" Monique said. "He's *beautiful!*"

I've yet to meet a cat that doesn't respond to sincere flattery. Bono spun around, tossed his mane and flashed his eyes at Monique. She called softly to him. He straightened his tail and strutted toward her.

To my amazement, he leapt onto the sofa between us. Purring lightly, he wrapped himself around Monique's hand. The chemistry between woman and cat was immediate and powerful; almost as if this was a moment they'd both been waiting for.

"I don't mean to sound strange," Monique said as Bono sprang onto the coffee table. "But do you believe in reincarnation?"

I struggled for an answer. Certainly, Lydia had unquestioning faith that souls were recycled through eternity.

"Something about him reminds me of Onyx," Monique continued.

Bono jumped off the coffee table and landed on her lap. Fixing her with those headlamp eyes, he meowed intensely at her.

"I thought so," Monique crooned back to him.

Goosebumps prickled up my arms. Any ambitions I had about keeping Bono dissolved. These two belonged together.

"How soon can I take him?" she asked.

I told her I'd need to contact Bideawee because there would be papers to fill out. No doubt they'd want to do a background check on her the way they had with me.

Monique said that was fine. She needed to talk to Berry first, anyway. Bono licked the back of her hand. Goosebumps prickled up my arms. Whatever her husband had to say about it, that woman and cat were meant for each other.

## Chapter Thirty-one

# HEALERS
# IN FUR

*A cat steps into a life
at the perfect moment.*

After Monique left, Bono nestled into my lap and draped his tail over my knee. Whenever the city became too loud and frantic, I'd come to rely on him as my anchor of serenity.

Though New York was dazzling, Bono had woken me up to the important things in life—kindness, love, patience, respect. He demonstrated it's possible to let go of past hurt and savor each moment with gratitude; that even a death sentence doesn't steal away the right to be playful. I couldn't imagine living in New York without him bouncing along at my side.

The more I thought about him and Monique, the less I pondered possible mystical connections between them. There was only one fairy god-mother in their story. Replaying conversations I'd had with Michaela, I realized she'd mentioned someone could be waiting in the wings several times. For some reason I'd just refused to listen.

Though I was full of hope for Bono, my insides ached at the thought of letting him go. He'd touched my heart in ways that would stay with me forever. I wasn't ready to say good-bye to him, New York, or Michaela and her inspiring friends.

I wondered if, given the chance to cool off, Monique might decide not to risk setting herself up for another heartbreak. Onyx had obviously meant the world to her, and she had implied he'd helped her through some tough experiences.

Time and again, I hear stories from people who've been emotionally rescued by their animals. When humans are crushed or in physical pain, four-legged champions seem to know they're needed at a profound level.

I'm always moved when readers write in to share how a special animal has impacted their lives. A woman who devotes her life to caring for her severely paralyzed son told me their Abyssinian cat is the only thing that makes him smile. She said she did not know how she or her son would cope without their cat's healing presence.

Another woman told me how heartbroken she was when her cat-loving sister committed suicide. At the funeral, she was astonished when a ginger cat appeared from behind a row of cypresses and circled the open grave. Tears melted into smiles when the feline leapt into the woman's arms. To her it seemed the cat was a messenger from beyond the grave. As she stroked the cat's fur, she could hear her sister's voice reassuring her, saying her anguish was over now and that some day they'd be together again.

A mother whose young daughter had died

wrote to say their cat Lily was her main source of healing.

The positive power of felines is experienced in every part of the world. From Seoul, Korea, to Atlanta, Georgia, cats are stepping into peoples' lives and going about their healing work.

Bono had helped me at a profoundly emotional level, too. He'd shown how wounds of the past are best forgiven and released. Much as I'd craved the thrill of living in New York, that little cat was living proof that the greatest excitement is to simply be alive and to glide into each day with an open heart.

I wasn't ready to part from him. Still, there was a chance Monique might visit Bideawee and find another, less needy feline. Or her husband might refuse to take on a cat with compromised health.

The deal was far from sealed.

## Chapter Thirty-two

# BRANDY AND BIG NOTING

*A cat can
be led astray.*

The author of *Love Story*, Erich Segal, couldn't have been more wrong when he wrote, "Love means never having to say you're sorry." Love means always saying sorry. Philip had been off the grid on a work retreat for a couple of days, but I figured he'd be back home by now. As soon as our time zones converged, I'd have another try at Skyping him.

Being the "least likely to stay married" couple had not always been easy, but it had compelled us to work harder for the relationship. Allowances had been made. He gave up encouraging me to train me for fun runs. I stopped trying to make him sing in tune. Most of our rifts were healed with laughter and chemistry. Whenever there were misunderstandings, we'd learned to let go and trust.

I pulled on my jacket and headed downstairs.

"Well, if it isn't Miss Holly Golightly!" an unmistakable voice echoed up the stairwell.

Patrick was in his usual position, leaning against his doorframe, cigarette dangling from yellowed fingers. Plodding down the stairs toward him, I waited for him to change my name to Helen Goheavily.

"Wasn't she some kind of call girl?" I said, trying to get the better of him for once.

When I first saw *Breakfast at Tiffany's* I was irritated by Audrey Hepburn's skittish character. Since watching my daughters grow through their twenties I recognized there's something of Holly Golightly in every young woman's struggle to find herself.

"Not at *all!* She was an American geisha," he said flicking a confetti of ash on the floor. "She came from some backward place to better herself in New York, just like you."

Patrick could hardly stop smiling at his own cleverness.

"And who does that make you?" I asked him. "Truman Capote?"

The author of *Breakfast at Tiffany's* claimed to have based Holly Golightly on several women. Others said the character was more like his mother, or even Truman himself.

Capote has been a quiet obsession of mine for years. In fact, if someone offered me a trip in a time machine, I'd go back to the Black and White Ball he hosted in New York's Plaza Hotel on November 28, 1966. Flush after the success of *In Cold Blood*, he threw the event in honor of *Washington Post* publisher Katharine Graham. There hasn't been an occasion like it before or since. The guest list ranged from Frank Sinatra and Gloria Vanderbilt to Lynda Bird Johnson and the Maharani of Jaipur. Though the champagne was Taittinger, the midnight supper consisted of scrambled eggs and sausages.

"I was thinking more the romantic lead in the film," Patrick said. "The man with the twinkling blue eyes. What was his name?"

"George Peppard."

Peppard was great in the movie. He looked at Audrey in a way only a straight man could. It was a terrible waste he went on to become a B-movie action hack. Still, even if this was Patrick's way of telling me he was straight, I wasn't about to find a guitar and serenade him on the fire escape with a rendition of "Moon River" as Audrey did for Peppard.

It didn't seem the right time to ask if he'd received my book. I rather hoped he hadn't. Instead, I told him how Mum used to sing "Moon River" at weddings.

"You mean people asked her to sing it?" he asked, bemused.

It's a mistake to tell another immigrant New Yorker about your past, unless you're incredibly close. Someone else always has a better story. Besides, the whole purpose of moving there is to shed history.

"They've made a million movies about New York, but nothing beats *Breakfast at Tiffany's*," Patrick said.

"I love how she stands in front of Tiffany's

shop window and tries to chomp through that Danish pastry," I said. "She must've been in a panic wondering how she was going to squeeze into that black Givenchy gown."

"I met him once," Patrick said.

"Who, George Peppard?"

"Truman Capote."

*"No!?"* If there was a law against name dropping, Patrick would be serving a life sentence.

"Well, not so much *met,*" Patrick added. "I handed him a coffee. Back in the seventies, I was working in the catering truck when they were filming *Annie Hall* in Central Park. Remember the part when Woody Allen says, "There goes the winner of the Truman Capote lookalike competition?"

I didn't, but nodded because it seemed a shame to break Patrick's flow.

"It was the real Truman Capote, you know. While he was hanging around waiting, someone told me to get him a coffee."

"What was he like?"

Patrick drew on his cigarette and exhaled plumes through his nostrils, giving him the appearance of a small dragon.

"Short," he said, after a long pause. "Now would you be coming in for that cup of tea?"

I hesitated. Even if Patrick had questionable intentions, he was a small man and I could probably fight him off. Still, the closest I'd ever come to being raped was by a very small man who turned out to be extremely wiry. That said, years of cigarettes and booze had taken their toll on Patrick's physique. On the other hand, there was a chance he might have a gun, or at the very least a kitchen knife. With any luck it would be quick, I thought. Besides, I'd survived about a month in New York with an unlocked window, which was the equivalent of lying on a railway track hoping there wouldn't be any trains.

The inside of Patrick's apartment was as dusty and worn as he was. Everything in it was gray or brown. He beckoned me to sit on a decrepit sofa whose imperfections were concealed under a moth-eaten tartan rug. Mounds of plates piled beside the kitchen sink. The air was heavy with cigarettes and stale whiskey. I glanced at the walls and couldn't help being charmed by the rows of old Penguin paperbacks. In the familiar shades of orange, red, yellow, and blue, their spines were pleated with use. A portable record player sat on top of a pile of ancient magazines and oozed Ella Fitzgerald singing "April in Paris." I made a mental note to avoid the bathroom.

He handed me a mug of tea with a gilt-edged handle. The mug itself was porcelain and decorated with a portrait of Queen Elizabeth, which he hastened to explain was ironic from his perspective.

From what I could work out, Patrick's life had been a patchwork. Aside from the jobs in hospitality (which was an oxymoron, he said, considering how naturally inhospitable he was), he'd done a bit of teaching. He'd had a go at writing, too. With all that, it was hard to imagine how he'd found the time to rub shoulders with so much greatness. Maybe it happened as a matter of course when a person lived long enough in New York.

When he asked if I'd be tempted by a whiskey, I shook my head.

"You'll be having a brandy then," he said in a voice so airy it couldn't be argued with.

It was a long time since I'd drunk brandy. The warmth surfed through my veins, unraveling knots of tension and arranging my whole body in a smile. Leaning back on a cushion of dubious pedigree, I wondered why I'd given up brandy. It was probably to fit in with Philip, who didn't enjoy the effects of alcohol.

Reading my mind, Patrick asked my opinion of the husband in *Breakfast at Tiffany's*. I thought it a sympathetic portrayal by the actor who went on to become Jed Clampett in *The Beverly Hillbillies*.

"But he was mad trying to drag her back to Texas," Patrick said, topping off my glass. "As if she was going to leave New York."

My eye wandered to a black-and-white photo

on the dust-laden mantelpiece. The two dark-haired men stood arm in arm, laughing into the lens. One was clearly a younger version of Patrick. The other had a softer, almost whimsical smile.

"Who's that?" I asked.

"Oh, just me and Frank."

"The *Angela's Ashes* guy?"

"Yes, that's right. Did I not tell you about him? Let me pour you another . . ."

## Chapter Thirty-three

# INVASION OF A DOOR SLAMMER

*A cat does not relish
being caught off guard.*

Dad used to keep a little bar in the corner of the living room. If I close my eyes, I can almost see the bottles gleaming on a silver tray. I liked the jolly Beefeater on the Gordon's Gin label, and the mysterious green of the Tanqueray bottle. There was always a specimen or two of Dad's Single Malt whiskey, and, alongside the cork-screw, a crystal decanter for sherry. People drank a lot of sherry in those days. My favorite was the soda bottle with a fitted lever, which could be squeezed to produce instant bubbles.

Hardly a night went by without a gin or whiskey being poured. There were parties, too. Tucked away upstairs, we kids slept through most of them, but we'd occasionally hear snippets about the time Mum danced on a tabletop or Dad ended up having to go to the hospital because he slashed his hand trying to fix the toilet.

Their behavior seems wild by today's standards, but going by *Mad Men* and the party scene in *Breakfast at Tiffany's*, they were normal by 1960s standards.

Mum and Dad made adulthood look like fun, and I was looking forward to it. By the time I understood a lot of their highs were alcohol fueled, I realized there were probably more constructive forms of enjoyment without the accompanying punishment of a hangover.

I sometimes wonder if Mum and Dad drank so much over their lifetimes, they left me with a mild allergy to the stuff.

The trouble with hardly ever drinking is how susceptible it leaves me to getting drunk. After two brandies, my cheeks were on fire. Patrick's apartment rotated around me in a movement that was almost imperceptible at first. Not since eating a three-course dinner in a revolving restaurant had I felt so queasy.

Glancing at my watch, I noticed the Skyping hour had arrived.

"You'll not be going now," Patrick said, as I made excuses.

I was still wary of telling him I kept an in-house animal. Through all my weeks of residency, I hadn't seen so much as a Pomeranian's tail in the building. Though he was entertaining enough, he had a dangerous tongue that thrived on gossip. The last thing Bono and I needed at this late stage was to be evicted by a building full of animal phobics.

"Let me see you out then," he said, sauntering toward the door.

The chill of the stairwell was a welcome balm. I heard the front door bang shut down at street level, followed by muffled voices. Our building was never silent.

*"Feel free to slam the door, won't you?!"* Patrick shouted into the stairwell.

His tone was so vitriolic I felt sorry for whoever was at the receiving end. But Patrick's mood was short-lived.

"Have yourself a glorious night, Miss Golightly!" he said, sweeping his arm with old-world panache in front of me.

His voice echoed across the stairwell. Leaning over the railing I inhaled gulps of tainted oxygen. That's when I noticed someone climbing the stairs below. He was wearing a black ski cap and a dark coat. Despite the suitcase he was dragging behind him, the man's stride was purposeful, almost athletic.

"Look what we have here," Patrick crowed. "A new arrival in earthly paradise!"

The man stopped and raised his head to look at us.

Most of the time, life spins past in such a blur the bulk of the day is forgotten by bedtime. This particular moment was different. As I looked down at the face, time slowed until it froze like an alpine lake.

Though I didn't recognize the ski cap, the strong jawline, the broad forehead, and steady blue eyes were instantly familiar. Philip was smiling up at me in that self-contained way of his. I galloped down the stairs and threw my arms around him.

"What are you doing here?" I said, barely able

to contain my happiness. "I thought you were on retreat."

He pulled me close and kissed me on the lips. It was unspeakably good to feel the warmth of his body.

"I decided they could manage without me for a while," he said.

It was unheard of. He never took time off from work. When I asked how he'd got into the building, he said he'd bumped into a nice woman from the first floor at the front door and she'd let him in.

"I wanted to surprise you," he added, refusing my offer to help him with the suitcase.

"You've certainly done that," I said, trailing after him up the flight of steps to Patrick's door. I was hoping Patrick would have had the tact and good manners to go back inside. But he was still standing in his doorway.

"You didn't say your son was paying a visit," Patrick said, narrowing his gaze through a shroud of smoke.

I corrected him. Philip extended his hand, enveloped Patrick's paw, and gave it a sturdy shake.

"So, you're the husband," Patrick said, after an appraisal. "Come to rescue Miss Golightly, have you? Good luck with that one."

If there'd been one of Patrick's whiskey bottles on hand, I'd have cheerfully clocked him with it.

## Chapter Thirty-four

# BUILDING BRIDGES

*To adopt a cat is to invite magic into your life.*

Bono greeted his second visitor of the day with interest. He sniffed Philip's suitcase and watched him unpack. I was pleased when the cat granted Philip a brief chin scratch. He remarked how small Bono was compared to Jonah, who'd gone to stay in Lydia's flat while he was away.

"But Bono has great personality," I said, as we watched his tail slide under the bed.

"I can see that," he said.

"He'll be friendlier when he gets to know you," I said, flinging arms around him again to make sure this wasn't a dream. "What made you come all this way?" I asked.

"Separation anxiety. My hair's falling out."

I laughed and stroked his head, which he'd taken to shaving in recent years.

"How is Jonah's leg?"

"The same. He misses you."

"I've missed you, too," I said.

"What have you missed?" he asked, kissing my nose.

"Tea and toast and bed."

"Is that all?" he asked, pressing closer against me.

"Maybe a few other things," I said, kissing his lips.

In fact, I'd missed everything about him—his steadiness, his kindness, his smell. Twenty-two years of shared history couldn't be erased in a single month.

Much as I'd like to report we spent the whole night entwined in each other's arms, the bed was too narrow for two adults to lie comfortably beside each other for an extended period. I'd forgotten his tendency to twitch and snore, while I try to sleep in the pose of da Vinci's *Vitruvian Man*. Around midnight, I pulled out Lydia's sheets and we flipped the sofa back into a bed.

Maybe it was the brandy, or the sheer delight of being together again, but I slept more soundly than I had for weeks. I woke next morning to find Bono watching over Philip from the sofa's back, the way he had with Lydia.

"How come you're still wearing your ski cap?" I asked.

"This place is freezing," he said.

He needed time to acclimatize.

Eager to share everything I'd learned to love about the city, I steered him through the traffic across Second Avenue for breakfast at the deli. He didn't seem to find the company of tired cops and manual workers as magical as I did.

"Do you think maybe next time we could go somewhere we don't have to weigh our food before we pay for it?" he said, folding his paper napkin and draping it over his half empty plate as if something had died under there.

"Sure," I said devouring the last of my porridge, scrunching my paper napkin into a ball and dropping it into my empty bowl.

I wanted the day to be perfect for him. Though he tolerates museums, he's an outdoor man at heart.

"What say we walk the Brooklyn Bridge?" I asked.

"Sounds great," he said. "There and back should be a good leg stretch."

"Actually, it's just over a mile long. And there'll be all sorts of extra footwork getting on and off the thing," I said. "How about we do a one-way walk?"

As the cab drove across to the Brooklyn side, I glanced up at the gothic arches raising their great steel ropes. Compared to today's skyscrapers, the bridge may seem modest. When it was finished in 1883, however, the towers dwarfed every other construction in America, and it was the longest suspension bridge in the world.

The Brooklyn vibe was more intimate and friendly than I'd expected. We strolled through a laid-back neighborhood and stopped for lunch at a hipster café. The whole point of a movement is to offend old people, and in that regard hipsterism fails. Having grown up in a household that kept chickens (organic because there was no alternative) and where Mum taught us to sew our own clothes, hipster ideals are as familiar as macramé wall hangings.

"Could you imagine living here?" I asked.

"Maybe," he said after a long pause.

"You could jog across the bridge to work in the mornings. Or maybe catch a ferry."

I had no idea if there was a ferry, but he'd always loved boats.

"That's just the point," he said. "I'd have to find a job here."

We walked hand in hand along the waterfront as the sun cast shafts of gold on the skyscrapers across the river. I thought of the millions of lives that had poured in and out of those concrete spires. Dreams had been made and shattered there, but the city itself was eternal. It was extraordinary that such an artificial creation could be so beautiful. If human beings can create New York, maybe there's hope for mankind.

It took a while to find the stairs to the bridge itself. A bridge is a symbolic connection between worlds. I occasionally dream of Sam waving good-bye before he turns away and steps onto a footbridge.

This time, however, crossing the Brooklyn Bridge with Philip felt like the merging of my two existences—with Bono in New York, and with him, Jonah, and our family in Australia.

"Are you serious about living here?" he asked.

"Maybe not forever," I said, peering up at the towers. "But . . ."

"I know. You're hooked on Bono. What's up there?"

"Peregrine falcons," I said. "I've heard they nest on the Brooklyn Bridge."

A love of birds is something we've always shared.

"You're joking!" he said. "Those things are the fastest animals on earth. They fly at 200 miles per hour. They could live anywhere."

"I know," I said. "They have all the freedom in the world, but they choose New York."

I could identify with those birds soaring across oceans to make their homes here. They nearly died out, but after DDT was banned in the seventies, they returned to the city.

"Falcons roost everywhere in New York—on tall buildings, church spires . . ."

"Have you seen any?" he asked.

"Not yet. I'm still looking."

"We have them in Melbourne, too, you know," he said.

"Peregrine falcons, really?"

"They had some roosting on top of Ramon's office building in the middle of the city," he said.

The sky turned pink and the wind spiked up as clouds clustered above the Empire State Building. Philip pulled his ski cap over his ears and smiled the way he does when he's feeling at home out in the elements. Though he'd visited New York a few times, it had always been on business. He'd never had a chance to drink the place in.

"I understand why you love it here," he said. "And that cat's pretty special."

"So, you think you could move here?" I asked.

My husband fell silent. He never says anything without thinking it through.

"We could try and work something out," he said.

Laughing with relief and love for my husband, I threw myself at him—and knocked him into the path of an approaching jogger.

That night the email came through. Monique wanted to adopt Bono.

## Chapter Thirty-five

# THE HAPPIEST GOOD-BYE

*A cat has no
use for tears.*

I'm a casual person. It's not that I don't appreciate people making an effort. It's just if something can be done with minimal fuss, I prefer doing it that way. Monique wanted to come to the studio as soon as possible to collect Bono, and I was happy to oblige. But when I phoned Bideawee with the good news, they were adamant we'd have to adhere to the adoption process rules, which turned out to be almost as formal as a marriage.

Bono sensed change in the wind. He lurked in his old hiding place and refused to come out. When Philip slid into the shadows on his stomach, Bono darted out the other side. After a few minutes' chase, the cat seemed to understand. He stopped running and lay on his side with his paws raised, almost asking me to pick him up.

Much as I'd dreaded the thought of wrangling him back into his carrier, Bono went out of his way to make things easy. He relaxed in my arms and allowed me to slide him in.

"It's okay," I said, gulping back tears. "You're not going back to prison."

Philip lifted the carrier while I packed Bono's food and medication into bags. I looped the cocoon bed through my elbow. Bono hadn't used it since he'd been sleeping on the pillow beside mine.

Blossoms on the trees alongside the East River had deepened to crimson since the first time Lydia and I had walked past the UN Building. The wind hadn't lost the edge to its tongue so my ski cap still came in handy. It seemed only yesterday we'd carried our precious cargo home from Bideawee. Lydia had wept then because Bono had a sad and limited future. Now a life brimming with love was waiting for him.

"This is an animal shelter?" Philip asked, when we reached the elegant building.

We sat quietly in the foyer while a wild-haired man argued with Jon over a dog he was determined to take home with him.

"I've been watching that dog for four hours and I want him *now!*" the man yelled.

In a calm voice Jon explained to the visitor that his background check didn't add up, that in fact the last time he'd adopted a dog it had ended up with the man's mother. On top of that, the man had given a false address.

"What are you saying? It's not false!" the man yelled.

"We've just put a call through to the number you gave and the woman we spoke to says you don't live there anymore."

The security guard shifted the weight on his feet as the man launched into another tirade and finally, to everyone's relief, left the building.

"Sorry about that," Jon said to us. "People don't always adopt animals for the right reasons. They want healing without giving back."

I was surprised how casually Jon acknowledged the healing power of animals. The depth of thought and care he put into his work was beyond anything I'd encountered. Our conversation was interrupted by a call from someone anxious to rehome an incontinent 14-year-old dog. Jon's patience was limitless, as usual.

From inside his carrier, Bono watched the parade of people, cats, and dogs passing by. I wondered if he recognized the place. If he did, he was giving nothing away.

I gripped the handle and rubbed a tear from my eye. All relationships end with good-bye. This one was happening sooner than my selfish heart would have liked. Bono had transformed New York City into a second home for me.

A flood of what-ifs washed through my mind.

"Let's go," I said, taking Philip's hand.

"What?" He seemed alarmed

"Let's take Bono and walk out of here right now."

"Are you sure?" he asked.

Patrick's words echoed inside my head: *Good luck with that one*. But my husband was no Doc Golightly. He'd hardly flown to New York to drag me back to life as a hillbilly. Besides, it was impossible to go "back." Even if I returned to Melbourne, it would be as a different woman.

As Philip leaned over to kiss my cheek, Monique and Berry arrived. Fantasies of abducting Bono dissolved in their laser beam smiles. I introduced them to Jon, who swept them away to his office to sign papers. When they emerged a few minutes later, Monique was glowing. Berry had the befuddled air of a new father.

"I thought we were taking a cat home for a trial," he said. "She didn't tell me we were *adopting* him!"

But when he saw Monique's smile, I could tell he wasn't going to raise a serious argument. He was a man who put his wife's happiness above all else.

"You can go now," Monique said to me, taking the cat carrier's handle.

*Who, me? Now?* I fought the instinct to snatch the handle back.

I peered into the cat carrier and rubbed Bono's nose through the wire.

"Be a good boy, won't you?" I whispered. "I love you."

That little black cat with the lion haircut had enriched my time in New York beyond words. Through him I'd met incredible people and experienced the soft heart of the city. His story had touched people around the world. I couldn't say good-bye.

"Are you crying?" Philip asked as we walked back along the East River.

"It's just the wind," I lied.

Philip wrapped his arms around me. I wept into his neck. Darling Bono. It was the best possible good-bye. Besides, I wasn't the first woman to cry over a cat.

## Chapter Thirty-six

# CROSSROADS

*A cat becomes a permanent
resident in the heart.*

Before she left New York, Lydia had made me promise to visit the Rubin Museum of Art, a gallery specializing in Buddhist masterpieces from Tibet and the surrounding countries. To my surprise, the Rubin was in Chelsea on West 17th Street and Seventh Avenue. Awash with sculptures and tapestries, the gallery's serenity was a world away from the bustle out on the streets.

Every married couple has a different protocol when it comes to viewing art. We're not the ones who walk hand in hand from artwork to artwork. Philip generally gives each piece an allotted amount of time and respect, whereas I flit from one to the next until I find something that speaks to me. If there's a seat nearby, I might happily absorb that one work for twenty minutes. To avoid discord, Philip and I usually take off in opposite directions to find each other forty minutes or so later near the exit.

I was drawn to a room where dozens of Buddha statues were displayed together. The space emanated such power it seemed to make time loop back on itself. A man sat in the corner meditating. Though I was tempted to join him,

I wasn't sure my knee would take kindly to the hard floor. I closed my eyes and tried to capture the energy of the room so I could report back to Lydia when we got home.

Afterward, it took a while to adjust to the change of pace on the street. We plunged into a shoal of shoppers and waited on a corner for the lights to change.

At first, I thought I imagined the voice calling my name. When I heard it again, louder this time, I ignored it thinking there must be a million Helens in New York.

A hand grabbed my shoulder. Startled, I turned to see Monique's dazzling smile. I could hardly believe it.

"How's Bono?" I asked, adjusting to the shock of seeing her.

"He's great!" she said, slightly breathless from chasing after me.

"Is he eating? Is he taking his pill okay?" I asked, aware of the anxious note in my voice.

To my relief, she nodded.

"He's not hiding all the time, is he?" I asked.

"No, he's very friendly," Monique said.

I felt a little crestfallen. It sounded like Bono wasn't missing me. When relationships end, I'd heard women talk about flings they have with "Transitional Men," who help them gain confidence so they can move on to Mr. Right. In Bono's case, I was Transitional Woman and

Monique was Mrs. Right. Though I felt a little sad, I knew it was how things needed to be.

Chances of our paths crossing like this were slimmer than a cat's whisker. Perhaps the meeting had been arranged on a spiritual realm between Bono, Lydia, and the Buddha statues.

The crowd swirled around us as Monique and I embraced each other on the street corner. For a moment it seemed we were in some kind of movie.

"I thank you every hour," Monique said.

The feeling was more than mutual. Monique was the saint Bono had been looking for. After the lights changed, Monique and I said good-bye.

"Let's go somewhere quiet," Philip said, guiding me into a taxi and directing the driver to head uptown.

Central Park was decked out in her summer greens. His built-in compass led us to a silky pond where model yachts admired their reflections as they glided across the water. If we were vacationing in Hades, he'd still find a boat to look at. We sat on a bench while a young street performer carved out intricate strains of Bach on his violin.

"Beautiful, isn't it?" he said, squeezing my fingers.

People probably thought we were quaint holding hands after twenty-two years of marriage. But we didn't do it for their benefit. I couldn't imagine life without the weight of his hand in mine.

"Didn't John and Yoko live somewhere around here?" I asked.

"I think you'll find the Dakota building's out of our range," he said with a smile.

With Yoko being seven years older than John, their age difference was similar to ours. Except Yoko didn't have two kids from a previous marriage in tow.

It takes a man of exceptional heart to embrace and raise stepchildren the way Philip had. He'd been equally tolerant and understanding about my two-thirds life crisis, if that's what it was.

"I don't need to live in the Dakota building," I said.

"Are you thinking somewhere closer to Michaela?"

"No," I said. "I love New York, but having you here has made me realize it's time I gave up fantasizing about other people's lives."

"Really?"

"The one we've created together is precious enough," I said. "It's taken decades of painstaking work from both of us."

The violinist was working himself into a Bach-induced frenzy. Philip stood and walked toward him.

"We'd be crazy to leave the kids," I said.

The musician's face lit up as Philip spoke to

him and dropped a dollar in the open case lying on the ground.

"I want our granddaughters to know us, and for us to help them grow into teenagers, don't you?"

Philip took my hand.

"And I need to say sorry."

"What for?" he asked.

"I don't know what happened after I was sick," I said. "The walls pulled in around me and I froze up emotionally. Maybe I thought I was dying. Then I met Bono."

Philip smiled.

"He's sicker than I ever was," I said, dabbing my eyes. "Bono taught me the whole point of being alive is to keep on loving no matter what."

Philip rested his arms on my shoulders and drew me to his chest.

"I've been shallow and self-centered," I said. "Please forgive me. There are so many layers to love. We haven't explored half of them. I'd like to keep on doing that with you, if you'll have me."

"There's nothing I want more," he said, hugging me tight. "But there's just one thing."

"What's that?"

"Let's make the next adventure a joint one," he said.

"Sounds wonderful!"

After we kissed, he led me through a tunnel of willows.

## Chapter Thirty-seven

# MOVING TO THE GROOVE

*Some cats would rather dance in the dark.*

Our last night in New York was tinged with sadness. Michaela and Gene invited us to go dancing with them at Iguana on 240 West 54th Street, just a few doors down from where the legendary Studio 54 wowed the world back in the disco era. It's a theater now, but in those days, if you were gorgeous enough to receive approval from the extremely picky doorman, you'd rub shoulders with everyone from Andy Warhol and Liza Minnelli to Elton John and Salvador Dali. For one New Year's Eve party, four tons of glitter were famously dumped on the floor, which is excessive even by disco standards. People grumbled that it took months to shed the sparkles from their clothes. After our experience with the Indian paint throwers, I can sympathize.

Michaela assured me Iguana would be nothing like Studio 54. It would be a casual get-together featuring sixties music without the rigors of contra dancing—and no glitter. She was right. Brick walls and low lighting ensured a relaxed atmosphere.

The dancers were another matter. New York is brimming with people who take their dancing very seriously. They have ordinary jobs by day, but at night they morph into Gene Kelly, Patrick Swayze, or Michael Jackson. Though they're wonderful to watch, I prayed none of them would approach me. It's a myth that all a woman has to do is follow the man's lead. Ginger Rogers would agree.

As a kid, I went to creative dance classes for eight years. Our teacher encouraged us to dance for ourselves. It's a philosophy that can be applied to most things, and I'm grateful she was around when I was still a piece of human blotting paper.

Though I loved the way movement could make music surge through my body, I was never going to be a dancer worth watching.

I still dance from time to time, usually around 6 p.m. when the blinds are down, dinner is in the oven, and the house is empty except for the cat. One of my favorites is Lake Street Dive crooning "I Want You Back." Some people don't like the lyrics, but I think the song is an accurate portrayal of one of humanity's great weaknesses—wanting what you can't have. Lake Street Dive's lead singer, Rachel Price, has such a sultry voice, she gets my hips gyrating—though at a pace so sedate it could be described as medicinal.

Dancing with Philip is fun, but rocking and rolling with him is like being thrown into a giant blender. I was happy when the music slowed down so I could run a hand through my hair and check that the armpits of my shirt had not darkened to shades of embarrassment.

Motown has the sensuality of caramel sauce dripping over ice cream. It takes me back to when I was a teenager driven insane by sex hormones. I don't miss that feeling. Young people are beautiful, but I feel sorry they have to go through so many years in that condition. If I had the choice of being beautiful on the outside and messed up inside my head, or a walking wreck full of serene and grateful thoughts, I'd choose the latter. Getting older has countless compensations.

One of the best dancers was a stunning African American man. I watched in admiration as he rippled across the floor. To my horror, he approached and extended his hand. His sole motivation must have been pity for my clumsy, earthbound movements. When I explained that I couldn't dance to anything like his standard, he said of course I could and guided me onto the floor. He was endlessly patient as I stumbled against him, trying to tune into his rhythm. Just when we were starting to get in the groove, I tripped over his foot.

If only I could move like Michaela. She swiveled from her hips, like a panther. As I watched her and Gene swing into a rock and roll number, I was reminded of our first night with Lydia at the ice dancing performance. The rink at Rockefeller Center would be melted by now. There'd be umbrellas and tables where, not so long ago, the Zamboni had toiled. I smiled at how determined I'd been to foster a cat with minimal personality or, better still, no cat at all. Now it was hard to imagine New York without Bono.

Later that night, kissing Michaela and Gene good-bye, I tried to pretend we were going away for just a few days. The thought of leaving New York for good was too much. I couldn't thank her enough for introducing me to Bono. How she'd managed to wave her magic wand and find him an adoring home with Monique was beyond me.

"Don't you worry," Michaela said. "I'll be sending you regular updates on Bono."

Next morning, as the cab rumbled toward JFK, I drank in the city skyline. Somewhere in that mass of shimmering towers, Monique would be watching over Bono as he padded into a new day. Just off Times Square, I pictured Michaela and Vida sitting at their desks discussing another book by some other author. Over at the pet supply shop on Second Avenue, Bluebell would be preening herself on the counter while Doris rubbed her ears.

Meanwhile, the handbag salesmen would be setting up their stall on the corner, and the beggar with one leg would be turning his mind to the front steps of an unprepossessing building with a red door.

Along the river at Bideawee, Jon and his staff were no doubt welcoming a new batch of needy animals. With the warmer weather it would be kitten season by now.

Tears welled in my eyes. It had been a privilege to be part of New York's animal-loving community. I was going to miss them all. Thanks to Vida's and Michaela's determination, I'd been able to share Bono's story with the world.

"You'll be back," Philip said, leaning across the seat and stroking my hand.

It had been an easy decision to make in the end. New York and the people I'd met there were magical. I adored them, but nothing could surpass the promise of spending the rest of my life with a wonderful man who'd tolerated my quirks through two decades and yet still claimed to love me. There was no doubt I loved him back. Together we'd built a home and a family, who miraculously seemed to like us.

"Jonah will be pleased to see you," Philip said, as we boarded the plane.

"I hope he doesn't punish me for being away so long," I said clicking the safety belt over my lap.

"I'm sure he won't," Philip said.

As the engines roared, I felt a surge of excitement. It wasn't the thrill of leaving for the unknown this time, but the thought of returning to our family and a feline who were very much loved.

From my window seat, I gazed down at the forest of skyscrapers and imagined a small black lion cat somewhere down there.

Because of Bono, part of me would always be in New York.

## Chapter Thirty-eight

# FIVE GUARDIANS

*There's something wonderful about being owned by a cat.*

There have been enough significant cats in my life to count on the fingers of one hand. All five had excellent manners (when they chose to use them), a talent for enjoying life on their own terms, and an admirable capacity for affection.

The first was black and white with fur too long for convenience. Like many cats with Persian blood, he hated being manhandled, particularly by children. I could hardly blame him. If our body hair grew a foot long and giants tried to grab us, we'd feel the same way. We named him Sylvester after the cartoon cat who was the arch nemesis of Tweety Bird. Sylvester lived up to his namesake. He idled his afternoons away dozing on top of my budgie's cage. Poor little Joey froze on his perch and turned a brighter shade of green while the cat flicked his tail across the bars. Sylvester didn't have to be psychic to figure out Mum didn't like cats. In return, he pooped in her high heeled shoes whenever possible. It must have involved a lot of skill to position his posterior over her precarious six-inch heels. The pointy toes allowed little room for error. But he concealed his weapons artfully, and they had the desired effect every time. Sylvester taught me that the undercat, if he thinks creatively, can have power.

Dad's opinion of cats differed from Mum's. When he found a tabby kitten wandering around the gasworks one day, he bundled him up and drove him home in the backseat of our old Ford Zephyr. Once inside the house, the kitten cowered under an armchair. I longed for him to feel safe enough to show himself. When he finally did, I noticed the marking on his forehead formed an *M*. When I begged to call him Mickey, our parents were too distracted to put up an argument. My brother later pointed out Mickey had six digits on his front paws. In Europe, it's said polydactyl cats were often killed as witches' familiars. They were popular on ships, however, and Ernest Hemingway loved them. Years later, when we visited Hemingway's cats in Florida, they were beautiful and gloriously offhand. Though they were descended from literary aristocracy, I loved how they reserved the right to lie in the grass and behave like cats.

Mickey became my first soul cat. He seemed to know when I needed the warm touch of his fur. When I arrived home after another confusing day at school (*What's the point of algebra?*), he'd be waiting for me at the top of the steps on the veranda. He understood everything, and asked nothing in return. Mickey taught me there is no such thing as "just a cat."

After I'd nearly grown up and rushed into marriage, our older son Sam talked me into taking on a small black cat he named Cleo. When she stood over us after his death, I learned about the healing power of cats and their connection to other worlds.

Through living with these three cats I learned many things, including how to appreciate subtle energy forms. They taught me to respect body language, to read the light around animals and people. To demand something of a cat is to invite disaster. It's far better to soften your heart and let the relationship evolve.

I'd never imagined cats had a sense of destiny, but years after Cleo died, when I was recovering from cancer, my sister, Mary, took me to a pet shop. A crazy clown of a Siamese kitten scrambled up the wire, reached out his paw, and touched my hand. In that moment, I knew he was telling me to take him home.

Jonah is a writer's cat. He's been doing his job for ten years now, and he takes it seriously. After his morning pill and it's just the two of us, he trots around after me. If by mid-morning I'm still wandering the house with piles of laundry and other excuses not to work, he cuts in front of me and, with the expertise of a sheepdog, herds me into my study.

Once I've settled in front of the computer with a coffee, he emits a satisfied meow and leaps on my lap. Jonah snoozes there for the rest of the day, occasionally interrupting me to stroll over the computer keyboard, or wrestle with the printer cables. Whenever I'm writing, I prefer to shut myself off from the world, but Jonah won't hear of it. If there's a knock on the door, he scampers down the hall to find out who's there. He welcomes workmen, neighbors, and religious salesmen with equal enthusiasm. He's not so keen on younger visitors. One glimpse of a child and he's off to hide in his cat run.

We have long and vocal conversations. He has opinions about everything. In the evenings, Jonah isn't satisfied unless I'm sitting in the brown armchair and Philip's in the red one. If we break the rules and swap, our obsessive cat yowls in our faces until we exchange seats. He adores watching television, especially wildlife shows viewed from the best upholstered lap he can find, which is usually mine.

Living with Jonah has taught me to reconsider reincarnation as a concept. He's a human trapped in a cat's body.

The fifth significant cat in my life is Bono. My fantasy about fostering a dozy old tortoiseshell was laughable. A little rock star lion was the cat I needed. We found each other at a time when we were both a bit washed up and doubtful about the future. Bono reminded me that no matter how patchy the past has been, it's essential to greet each day with an arabesque and a purr. He introduced me to extraordinary people, and taught me that no matter how desperate a situation, there's a place for miracles.

From Bono I also learned that sometimes love means having to say good-bye.

## Chapter Thirty-nine

# WAITING
# FOR BONO

*A cat cannot cross the
same street twice.*

Michaela kept her promise and fed me regular updates of Bono's new life. No longer a shelter cat, he was living like a sultan with countless toys and a seven-tier scratching post. Under Monique's doting care, the only water he drank was purified. Black cats are notoriously difficult to photograph, but Michaela assured me he'd put on weight and his fur was glossy. I was delighted to hear that when people visited, Bono was quite the host these days. He'd also expanded his role to become a therapy animal, regularly staying with Monique's elderly parents, who adored him. Bono's new vet insisted he was closer to 8 than 5 years old. Most important, his health was excellent. Meanwhile, back at home, the fur on Jonah's leg had grown back.

I wasn't the only one hanging out for Michaela's reports. Since our time together in New York, Lydia and I were much closer. She'd moved into a townhouse with Ramon and they seemed very happy. Ramon tended a forest of pot plants, the closest they were allowed to a cat due to their landlord's animal ban. Whenever Lydia and I met, she'd be toting her jungle print handbag. I took it as secret code between us that whatever else happened, we'd always have Bono and New York.

Though Bono didn't need me anymore, I ached to see him again. Two years after our farewell, I found an excuse to return to New York in May 2015. I tried to book the old studio, but it wasn't available anymore. After several wild goose chases, I settled for a place on the Upper East Side. It belonged to Dan, who was keen on water sports, which could mean anything these days.

Even though it was late at night, the cab driver seemed to know exactly where to take me this time. He glided to a halt outside an old terraced building in what seemed a civilized neighborhood. I clattered my bag up a few steps to enter my base for the following week. Decorated in shades of brown, it was an exact replica of the photos I'd seen on the website. There was the luxury of a separate living room, and the bedroom opened onto a small, paved courtyard. A row of cushions sat on the bed under a huge photograph of a wave that threatened to unfurl any moment and swamp the room. I put it down to Dan's surfing interests. A hint of shampoo hovered in the air. I almost missed the raffish smell of the old place.

After I'd changed and slid between the sheets, a man's voice started up on the other side of the wall. He was on the phone sharing details of his workday with someone called Darling. It seemed his office was overflowing with demons and narcissists. Corporate politics is the same the world over. After what seemed hours, he told Darling how much he loved and missed her, and we were all able to get some sleep.

I woke the next morning to hear my neighbor talking to Darling again. He'd slept well, thank you, and hoped she had too. He told her to have a wonderful day, that he'd be thinking of her every minute of it, and he loved her so much. Mwah, mwah.

Making comparisons between your own relationship and other people's is pointless. Other couples may seem devoted to each other, but it's easy to put on a show in public. Then again, unless they had a weird kink about people listening in on their phone calls, what I was hearing was just between the two of them. I smiled at the thought of them being in the throes of a new love. Diamond rings and wedding cakes . . . nothing could be more romantic.

After my neighbor had left for work, I unlatched the French doors. It wasn't the grandest courtyard, but on a mild spring morning I wasn't about to waste it. I negotiated tubs of withered plants and stood on tiptoe to inspect next door, but the fence was like the Great Wall of China. There weren't any cracks to peer through. I shifted a rickety seat into a shaft of sunlight. A bird warbled a tentative melody from a nearby tree. With a cup of coffee and the *New York Times*, I was practically in paradise.

To fill in the hours before I could see Bono and Michaela, I wandered tree-lined streets. The Upper East Side is a world away from Midtown. Nannies of various ethnicities shouted into their phones while they pushed oversized strollers containing kids easily old enough to get around on their own two feet. A diminutive doorman escorted a teenager twice his size onto the sidewalk and helped the hulk adjust his backpack.

I was taken back when a limo glided past with a pale-faced boy in the back. With his school uniform and neatly parted hair, he was a clone of Richie Rich. It hadn't occurred to me the comic-book character I'd grown up with could have been based on a real boy.

Two limos later, I realized the Upper East Side is populated by hundreds of Richie Riches. Yet in all this opulence, it seemed a type of apartheid was going on. I had the impression those who served were not only taken for granted but invisible to their employers. Around a corner, a group of African American kids gathered around a portable soup kitchen.

With there being so many different ways to live in New York, I was grateful for the weeks I'd had with Bono in a scruffy studio near Grand Central. That little lion cat had opened the door to the city's soul for me. Though I knew New York could be a tough place to live in, I'd always think of it as a warm and generous place because of him.

Much as I loved the city, it was right for me to live with Philip, our family, and crazy Jonah. The world's a small place these days, anyway. I consoled myself with the thought that New York and Melbourne are never more than a day apart.

Wandering past smart restaurants and nail salons, I pretended to enjoy myself. But I couldn't wait to see Bono.

## Chapter Forty

# OLD HAUNTS

*A cat feels at home
when she is invisible.*

My heart sank when Michaela told me Monique and Berry had gone away for a couple of days. The Bono reunion was on the back burner.

With her usual sixth sense, Michaela invited me out to a night of my dreams—dinner at the Algonquin Hotel followed by a Broadway performance of *An American in Paris*. For years I'd been in awe of the Algonquin and the witty circle of writers who met for lunch there every day throughout the 1920s. Fortunately, the hotel has maintained enough dark wood and carpet to keep the ghosts of Dorothy Parker, Harold Ross, Robert Benchley, and the rest alive.

Michaela and Gene were waiting for me in the foyer. As we threw arms around each other it felt as if we'd been apart for five minutes rather than two years. Whenever our kids fret over losing friends who are moving away, I assure them distance has little impact on true friendship. Besides, intermittent catch-ups with people you have a shared history with is, like the finest cognac, all the more treasured for its rarity.

"Have you met Matilda?" Michaela asked.

Casting the name through a mental list of her friends and colleagues, I couldn't think of a Matilda.

Michaela pointed across the room at a gray and white Ragdoll cat who was busy greeting guests.

"The hotel cat," Michaela said. "There's been a Matilda at the Algonquin since the 1930s. Different cats, of course, but the same name. Unless it's a male, and then it's called Hamlet."

"How Shakespearean," I smiled.

"Well, we are in the theater district," Michaela said. "And it was an actor who suggested the name."

I crossed the room and bowed before Matilda. My homage was acknowledged by a regal lick on the back of my hand.

"Matilda has her own Facebook page," Michaela said.

Of course. What self-respecting hotel executive wouldn't?

I've always loved Gershwin, and *An American in Paris* was a delicious concoction. The dancers reminded me of Bono and how his feet barely touched the floor. Watching a young man flex his spine backward, I winced and hoped he wasn't lining himself up for arthritis a few years down the road. When I was younger, I used to think dance and acrobatics was to do with showing off. These days, I watch openmouthed and wonder how a human body can do such things.

I caught a cab back in time to listen to my neighbor saying goodnight to Darling . . . *you*

*hang up first . . . go on . . . love you . . . are you
still there? . . . Oh. No,* you *hang up!*

One of the traits I identify with cats about is
their invisibility. Compared to roughly 85 million
cats in the United States, there are only about
75 million dogs. Cats are tucked away in houses
and apartments. They observe the world from
the top of garden walls or from under hedges.
Cats spy on people, but we seldom see them.
They're the tail disappearing behind a fence,
the curtain twitching inside a window. Aware of
others' sensitivities, cats take pains to leave no
trace. Dogs, by contrast, demand center stage.
They dump on the sidewalk on the assumption
someone else will deal with it. On the streets
of the Upper East Side, it seemed every third
person was escorting a tiny pedigree on a leash.
I stopped outside grooming parlors to watch
dogs getting outlandish haircuts. The window of
a doggie day care framed a restless sea of pugs
and Pomeranians, miniature poodles, and terriers.
A tired-looking woman trailed after them with a
mop. She wasn't about to win Happiest Employee
of the Year.

Last time I was in New York, I didn't have to
take the subway seriously. Living on the Upper
East Side was a different matter. Provided I
stayed clear of rush hour, I found the subway
system endearingly archaic and almost spacious
compared to Tokyo's. I read somewhere it's

advisable to avoid eye contact with other passengers, but that applies to just about any transport system these days.

After getting off at Grand Central, I wandered past familiar shops and boxes of orange tulips up to Second Avenue. It was always spring in New York. There was so much I'd missed—the rumble of trains under my feet, the steam gushing from grates and manholes as if the city was about to erupt any second. And the fire hydrants. Every other city I know has fire hydrants you wouldn't look twice at, but New York's are miniature works of art. I stopped off at the bakery where Lydia and I had demolished a pastry with a million calories. I ordered one for old time's sake, which was a crime seeing there was no one to share it with. Like someone haunting the scene of an ancient love affair, I made my misty-eyed way up to the corner of 44th. Once the handbag sellers had assessed I wasn't a potential customer, they turned their backs. Outside our old building the same old beggar was sunning his stump on the steps and munching something out of a paper bag. I wished I'd been bold enough to make friends with him when I'd been living there.

Standing on the sidewalk and gazing over his head up at the red door with the heart-shaped lock, I almost felt like I was home again. Though the neighborhood was achingly familiar to me, I was back to being an outsider. Even if I could work out which buzzer belonged to Patrick, he'd probably forgotten me. I had not caused a ripple on the surface of his existence. In two years, nothing and everything had changed. Bono and I did not live there anymore.

## Chapter Forty-one

# LIVING LIKE A CAT

*Things Bono
taught me.*

Hope of seeing Bono again was fading. I decided it was probably a good thing. He had a new life now and certainly wouldn't remember me. Besides, I had no right to barge into Monique's world and claim any part of him.

Michaela had told me not to miss the cat exhibition at the Japan Society of New York on 333 East 47th Street. The Japanese have long loved cats, and some of the woodblocks were centuries old. Intimate domestic scenes depicted felines in every mood—from fierce hunter to furry plaything. I was drawn to the philosopher cat sitting on a window ledge gazing at Mount Fuji. Cats accompany people through every phase of their lives.

On a recent visit to Japan, nothing could have prepared me for the devastation near Sendai where the tsunami had risen up and swallowed the countryside in 2011. Years after the event, I was awestruck by the vast tracts of coastal land that were still uninhabitable. Thousands of people remained homeless and grieving for lost ones. Though the scale of loss was greater than anything I'd experienced, I found many people wanted nothing more than to share their stories.

It's such a basic need, I wondered if arranging tragic events into a logical shape is a way of helping the brain adjust to trauma. At a human level, I felt honored every time a stranger from this cultivated and restrained society wanted to share their pain. Often, all people need is for someone to listen deeply with compassion.

One of the unspoken horrors of the tsunami was the loss of so many animals. Perhaps there had been one or two miracles like Bono's, but in most cases there was no time, no hope to rescue them. My hosts showed me more graves than I'd seen in a lifetime. Incense hovered over rows of gleaming black headstones. An old man bent to place yellow chrysanthemums on a grave. A small family group gathered in silent tears around another.

Many people who have survived ill health and tragedy remind me of cats. Like Bono in his cage at Bideawee, they accept they may have to spend a long time imprisoned in grief. That doesn't stop them bouncing out to chase a sock occasionally. It's almost as if the harrowing experiences they've been through have equipped them to savor the delight of being alive,

Though Bono's future was limited, he wasn't wired to worry, or to fret over how things might have worked out differently if he hadn't lost his home in Hurricane Sandy.

The lion cat greeted the morning sun

with curiosity each day. Every moment was brimming with adventure for him. Whether it was a cockroach or a fluffy toy cat, he was not disappointed.

To Bono every day was a good one, simply because he was in it. He could be mesmerized by a reflection of light on the wall, and spend hours chasing a scrunched up ball of paper.

Bono knew how to look after himself. He spent hours grooming and rearranging his lionish haircut, followed by an afternoon's sun baking on his favourite white cushion with the black polka dots.

Yet Bono stayed connected to his wild side. He was resilient and could outsprint me whenever he felt like it.

He was slow to make assumptions about people and, if necessary, fast to disappear.

Though it took me a while to discover this, Bono knew how to love. He was brave, too. No matter what cruelty he had suffered in the past, he still had enough residual trust to embrace Lydia, and later me, with great affection.

He was a good listener.

Bono was willing to forgive and move on. He understood life is always changing and ultimately you have to flow with it.

He knew life is precious because we are all fragile, and our presence on Earth fleeting. He was too engaged with living to worry about dying.

Through the anxious days after the Boston bombings, Bono knew I needed comforting. I didn't have to ask for his warmth and companionship. He made sure I never felt alone. He was never "too busy" to help a friend.

Bono approached each moment from a place of gratitude, which gave him strength and natural grace. Because of that, people warmed to him. Then the people who liked Bono started warming to each other.

At night, he sat on the window ledge and gazed up at the moon and wondered at the miracle of being alive.

Like all felines, Bono had great style. Whatever happens, I aim to spend the rest of my life living like a cat.

## Chapter Forty-two

# I REMEMBER YOU WELL

*Rescue cat
becomes rock star.*

Just when I'd accepted Bono and I weren't meant to see each other again, Michaela called with a breath-stopping invitation.

She said Bono would be delighted to host drinks at Monique and Berry's apartment, followed by dinner for us all at hers. Not since my audience with the Dalai Lama had I felt so happy and nervous at the same time.

There's so much to love about the Chelsea district where Michaela and Monique live. A happy soup of immigrants, gays, and creative types give the place a tolerant bohemianism. Like every corner of New York, the neighborhood has more than its share of fame. Look no farther than the redbricked Chelsea Hotel on 222 West 23rd. Dylan Thomas was staying there when he suffered a terminal case of pneumonia in 1953. Years later, the body of Sid Vicious's girlfriend, Nancy Spungen, was found in a room. Mark Twain, Tennessee Williams, and Charles Bukowski all sweated ink inside its walls.

The doorman inside Michaela's building greeted me with a smile.

"We've been expecting you," he said, pointing me at a comfortable chair in the lobby while he called her up to announce my arrival. This building was worlds away from the scruffy studio Bono and I had hung out in. No wonder Michaela had seemed a bit shocked when she visited us. When she appeared and escorted me to the elevator, I was almost overwhelmed with nervousness.

"Is he still scared of strangers?" I asked as the elevator sighed shut.

There's only so much a person can ask of a cat. I was well aware the whole human-cat relationship is based on whether or not a cat is inclined to engage with you. Not the other way around.

For me, Bono had transformed New York into a home with a heart on the door. If there's such a thing as "meant to be together," we'd been it for that magical month. I loved him as much as I did back then, but no way could I hope for any form of acknowledgment now. As a form of protection, I repeated the mantra "he's not going to recognize you" over and over inside my head.

"He usually greets me at the front door," Michaela said.

That didn't sound like the same animal who used to scurry under a bed at the rattle of a door handle. I held my breath as we stepped out of the elevator. Across the corridor, a door creaked open a crack. I waited for Monique to appear. Instead, down at ground level, the head of a noble black feline emerged. With the confidence of a lord, he pushed the door open. Tail aloft in greeting, he padded toward us.

"This can't be Bono!" I whispered, crouching on the floor and offering my hand.

To my delight, he stepped forward and honoured me with a gracious nudge. If indeed it *was* Bono, he no longer sported a lion haircut. His coat was a gleaming curtain. Exquisitely groomed and glowing with health, this animal was worthy of a blue ribbon in anyone's pet show.

I hesitated. This had to be some kind of joke the two women had cooked up. Most likely Monique kept more than one cat, and the real Bono was cowering in a corner somewhere inside the apartment.

Just when I was about to call Michaela's bluff, the cat raised his head and fixed me with a pair of amber traffic-light eyes. They were bright and clear. The unhealthy-looking oily film I used to worry about had disappeared. The magnificent creature emitted a musical mew. He then turned and stretched his back leg in an unmistakable arabesque.

Bono may not have recognized me, but Monique and Berry did. We exchanged hugs and laughter as their feline master strolled through their apartment. This home betrayed the obsessions of its owners. Aside from the seven-tier cat tower I'd heard about, the place was scattered with catnip toys and fishing lines. Monique and Berry's apartment had the trappings of an entire pet shop—all for one cat.

None of us could take our eyes off Bono as he settled himself into a cardboard box.

"He loves boxes," Monique said.

I felt a jab of regret. Bono and I hadn't been together long enough for me to discover he had a thing for boxes. Heaven knows, if anyone had told me, I'd have found him twenty. On the other hand, maybe he'd needed the security of Monique's love in order to let go and relish the joy of cardboard. My mixed emotions dissolved when I saw the transformation in him. The scrappy little rescue cat had morphed into a rock star.

"He's such a friendly little guy," Monique said. "And his health is great."

The proudest of mothers, Monique smiled down at Bono.

"When Monique and Berry go away Bono sometimes stays with my three cats upstairs," Michaela added.

"That's if my parents will let him," Berry said. "They never taught us about therapy cats in med school. But Bono's definitely become one for my parents. They're always asking if he can stay with them. They adore him. It's really opened my eyes to the power of therapy cats."

I was delighted Berry's devotion was so evident considering he'd been half tricked into adopting Bono. Maybe like most men, he'd taken a little longer to get the hang of parenthood.

After a glass of wine, we left Bono to ride the elevator up for dinner at Michaela's. Not for the first time, I was impressed by how comfortably New Yorkers have adapted to living vertically. Gene greeted us and poured more wine, as I stood momentarily speechless in front of the view from the living room window.

The Empire State Building felt almost close enough to touch. To one side of it, the tip of the Chrysler Building peeked out like a cheeky cousin. Apricot-tinged clouds gathered high above rooftop gardens. I smiled at the quirky wooden water towers nestling on top of almost every building. Shaped like medieval haystacks, they give the skyline a whimsical air but, as every New Yorker knows, their function is twenty-first century. Every building taller than six stories must have a tower and pumping system to provide water pressure.

Mesmerized by a stream of red taillights crawling up Eighth Avenue, I asked Michaela what her favorite time of day was to soak up this spectacle. She put her head to one side as though she'd never thought about it before.

"After dark's amazing with all the lights," she said, "But then I love dawn when the city's quiet and people haven't started going to work."

I tried to imagine the view without the taillights. "Winter's magical, too," she added. "The buildings are shrouded in mist."

I began to appreciate there's never a bad time to live with a panorama worthy of a jigsaw puzzle. On top of that, I quietly noticed her apartment passed my "walk around naked" rule.

Once I'd managed to disconnect my eyeballs from the view, Michaela introduced me to her fur family, all three of them rescue cats who could hardly believe their luck.

"Meet Belle Amie," Michaela said, holding up a white female with gray and yellow blotches and a pretty pink nose. "I adopted her as a kitten in 2003. She's my Snuggle Queen, aren't you girl? She sleeps between my knees every night."

I followed Michaela to a bedroom where Alcatraz, a handsome white male with black markings and a fluffy tail, was sprawled over a blanket at the foot of the bed.

"There's Alcatraz," she said. "He moved in when he was six weeks old back in 2008. That's his personal blanket. He sleeps there by my feet every night. He's highly strung. I call him my ear scratch addict."

There was no doubt who was ruling this roost.

"And look out. Here comes Ranger!"

A small yellow and white tiger bounded toward us.

"She's the boss of the household, aren't you

Ranger?" Michaela said, gathering the cat into her arms. "This one's duty-bound to shred every paper towel and toilet paper roll in her path, aren't you girl?"

Ever since Ranger moved in back in 2014, she'd been sleeping near Michaela's left shoulder, close enough to take the occasional chomp of her hair.

It made me wonder how I could have grumbled about sleeping under one cat. Michaela spent her nights buried in them.

The sky darkened and the city became a glittering spectacle while we scraped our plates clean. It was such a beautiful evening, brimming with affection and happiness, part of me wanted to capture it and put it in a bottle like one of Mum's peaches. But I was finally learning that an essential art of life is allowing wonderful moments (as well as the not so good) to pass with grace. As I thanked everyone and prepared to leave, Monique asked me if I'd like a few moments alone with Bono. I quickly agreed and took the elevator back downstairs with her.

"There you go," she said, unlocking her front door. "I'll just wait out here."

When I stepped inside, Bono was dozing in the cardboard box.

"Hello, old fella," I said, bending and moving slowly toward him.

He shook his sleepy head. I asked him if he

remembered Lydia and our shabby old studio.

"You're living like a king, these days, aren't you?" I said, offering my hand. He raised a regal chin to accept a scratch.

"What about the time you bolted up the fireplace?" I said, tears suddenly streaming down my cheeks. "What were you thinking?"

Bono dipped his head and hummed a tinkling purr. I ran my hand over the lush carpet of his spine and was heartened to discover the sharp edges of rib cage had been well padded out.

"It doesn't matter if you don't recognize me," I gulped, swiping tears off my chin. "I'm so happy for you."

I kissed the top of his head and stood up. As I walked toward the door to join Monique, something made me turn around to take one last look.

Some say cats show affection for humans with a leisurely blink otherwise known as an eye kiss. When Bono gazed up at me and blinked those owlish eyes, an electric exchange took place between us. As he beamed me golden halos of affection, I knew he was telling me he hadn't forgotten our time together, and that he was grateful for his new life. It was then I heard words I hadn't expected or hoped for, but they came across clearly, and in the kindest voice: "You can go home now."

## Chapter Forty-three

# ISLANDS APART

*A tale of
two cats.*

After my second trip to New York, extraordinary things happened. First, the ants disappeared. I've no idea why, apart from the fact they had been with us so many years I'd forgotten to hate them, which proves my theory about enemies needing hatred to feed off.

Secondly, with a few physio sessions and Pilates, my knee fixed itself.

Then we did something I'd always said would be the last thing I'd ever agree to. We fulfilled Philip's dream of buying a beach house, complete with a runabout boat. It's a dishevelled 1960s shack on Phillip Island (with two *l*s, unlike my husband). About two hours' drive from Melbourne, the island has never been fashionable, which I consider in its favor. Though it's slightly larger than Manhattan, it has only 11,000 permanent residents. Like Manhattan, it's connected to the mainland—in this case, by a single bridge a third of a mile long. As with New York, a certain degree of eccentricity is tolerated on the island. Safe to say comparisons end there.

Home to surfers, farmers, environmentalists, and a few artists, the island has a rugged beauty that reminds me of the coastal area where I grew up in New Zealand. Untamed surf beaches give way to sheltered golden ones.

I like the down-to-earth islanders, the clear salty air, and the way waves roll up from Antarctica to smash themselves on the rocks. But the main reason I love the island is it's one of those rare places where wild animals have paid humanity the compliment of sticking around. The ocean is alive with thousands of seals and penguins. Native Cape Barren geese with lime green beaks strut the roads safe in the knowledge anything on wheels will stop for them. Wallabies pay regular visits to our backyard.

When we wake in the mornings to the squawk of black cockatoos, I lie still and wait for the sound of jam being scraped on toast. I've realized few things could be more romantic than a husband of two decades bringing his wife tea and toast in bed. To think I wasted so long arguing against his beach shack dream. Sure, it means there are extra beds to make sometimes, but visitors bring their own sheets, and there's always someone around to pick up a tea towel. Lydia and Ramon generously donated a robotic vacuum cleaner that swivels across the floor collecting the sand I'd fretted about. As for Jonah, he's happy to exchange two hours on the backseat in his cat carrier for a long weekend sprawled in the sun on the back of a sofa at the beach.

The old house seems to have expandable walls

that, when Philip's dad visits from New Zealand, happily accommodate four generations. Through the cycle of Christmases and birthdays, I watch our granddaughters soak up moments they'll remember into their twilight years.

Some of my favorite times are when it's just the two of us (plus Jonah), and the house draws around us in an embrace. Once Philip's checked the tides and the sea is looking tame enough, I will help him launch his boat. Out on the water, the working week peels away from his face and I see the man I fell in love with all those years ago—and still am.

When a dolphin rises from the crest of a wave and greets me with a curious eye, I realize I don't need to worry about growing old. All that matters now is to keep on growing up.

Nights can be chilly on the island. After a glass of red wine in front of a blazing log fire, we tumble into bed with Jonah hot on our heels. As we nestle between the sheets, I reach for the fluffy warmth of Philip's flannelette pajamas. Somehow, green tartan is a perfect match for the island. In fact, they fit into these surroundings so well, I bought myself a red pair to match.

An Aboriginal man once told me people leave a silvery trail wherever they go through life. Even after someone has left a place and moved to another, traces of her spirit remain. Part of me will always belong in New York with Bono, and in New Zealand as well as other corners of the world I love. If I could have a thousand lives, I'd commit to every one of them and make them home. For now, all I have is this life, this moment.

Bono reminded me to live with optimism and great heart. Like him, I try not to waste time dwelling on what I've lost and how little time I have left. Fear is irrelevant. Where we've come from and where we're going aren't so far apart.

I walk barefoot along the beach and savor the waves washing like iced champagne over my toes. With family, friendships, and an enduring marriage, life is complete. Thanks to Bono, I'm not restless anymore. A forever home is beyond price.

# *Acknowledgments*

It takes more than one person to create a book, and in this case *Bono* has hundreds of guardian angels. Without the unwavering devotion of Michaela Hamilton and Vida Engstrand to rescue cats, I would never have encountered the rock star cat or met the dedicated people who work at Bideawee.

Philip has been incredibly generous in encouraging me to write this book. Through the year I was working on it, he demonstrated limitless patience reading the latest pages aloud every night. Not only did this give him the opportunity to veto the worst of my transgressions, it helped me find a sense of rhythm in the sentences.

My sister, Mary Dryden, in New Plymouth, New Zealand, has also been wonderfully supportive reading extracts of the book. Like the best of big sisters, she never criticized but kept asking, "What happens next?"

Huge thanks to my daughter, Lydia Brown, for being part of the Bono story. I've never seen her so moved by an animal, and I'm sure some day she'll fulfil her dream of having a rescue cat.

The first time I wrote about her, I was about to give birth to her, so she's had a lot to put up with through the years.

A big hug to our younger daughter, Katharine Gentry. I treasure her ceaseless optimism about what I do—not to mention her astute editorial eye. I can't thank Kath enough for her kindness and care helping me recover from surgery while I was working on this book.

To son Rob, his wife Chantelle, and their daughters Annie and Stella, I love the times we spend together (even if I can't stand up as fast as you, Stella). You enrich my life more than you know.

Without my extraordinarily talented Australian editor, Jude McGee, I'd most likely still be in the supermarket trying to decide between red potatoes or brown ones. Ten years ago, when Jude scooped the manuscript of *Cleo* off a pile and saw a glimmer of possibility in it, she changed my world.

I'm grateful to my agent, Anne Hawkins, for her stalwart support. Thanks, too, to Karen Auerbach, director of publicity at Kensington Publishers. And to the enormous number of people who, when they read about Bono on the *Huffington Post*, took his plight to their hearts. Their generous words meant a great deal through the bleak days when it looked as if he would never find a home.

Speaking of which, the greatest heroes of this story are Monique and Berry. Their kind-heartedness and compassion for a terminally ill animal is an inspiration. This book is my homage to them and all the saints who welcome lost and broken souls into their homes.

## Center Point Large Print
600 Brooks Road / PO Box 1
Thorndike, ME 04986-0001 USA

**(207) 568-3717**

**US & Canada:**
**1 800 929-9108**
www.centerpointlargeprint.com